Your Mess Matters. Exactly. Such a tru
power-packed book that will challenge,
in your own personal journey. Luke Lezon writes with refreshing vulnerability and connects deeply with an honest but often overlooked reality for all of us—we're all a mess! But with Jesus, that mess can be redeemed and transformed into something impactful.

Brad Lomenick, former leader of Catalyst

If you've ever been stuck, if you've ever struggled, if you've ever asked, "Why me?" make this book your next read! Luke Lezon invites you on his journey from mess to message to masterpiece. This incredible resource is filled with eternal truths from Scripture and a compelling story that empathizes with your pain. Find hope, healing, and even meaning in some of life's messiest moments.

Jonathan Pokluda, lead pastor of Harris Creek Church and former lead pastor of The Porch at Watermark Church

Luke and I have been good friends for many years now. He was arguably my biggest mentor leading up to my marriage. He was and is a man I turn to when I need help, but he's also just a good friend I've shared countless laughs with. I believe this book will help you through whatever it is you can't let go of, find yourself in, or will face in the future. If you've ever struggled, this book is for you. Luke writes with passion and power that leans on the Word of God. *Your Mess Matters* will help move you from the shame and pain you feel into the loving arms of Jesus.

Cole LaBrant, YouTube personality

The authenticity that Luke spills onto these pages is nothing less than soul-healing. People no longer want to read books from perfect Christians teaching them how to live perfect lives. They want to know that their mess matters and that God can bring them out of the mess. Luke delivers that perfectly in this new book.

Carlos Whittaker, bestselling author

I often tell our congregation that if we don't have problems and struggles, then Jesus has nothing to offer us. From His own words, we learn that Jesus did not come for the righteous but for sinners, not for the healthy but for the sick. If you have become convinced that you are sinful or sick, or for that matter weak, injured, aching, fearful, out of control, or worn out, then Jesus—as well as the book you hold in your hands that points to Him—can be of great benefit to you. Beginning with his own story, Luke does a fine job of introducing us to the One we call "The Great Physician."

Scott Sauls, senior pastor of Christ Presbyterian Church in Nashville, Tennessee, and author of several books, including *Befriend* and *Irresistible Faith*

In *Your Mess Matters,* Luke speaks from firsthand experience. I've walked through the messes of life, and Luke's words give me hope—a hope we can cling to no matter what our lives look like today. Whether you're in the middle of a mess right now or have gone through one in the past, I guarantee this book will meet you right where you are.

Adam Weber, pastor and author of *Talking with God*

We need more books that talk about the mess. We need more books like this one, where the author isn't afraid to get down in the trenches and record the faithfulness of God in the hard-to-share moments. This book will comfort you and remind you of the truth while giving you the assurance you need to keep powering through the journey. I'm more convinced than ever that the mess is precious and something we need to talk about. Let this book be the fire-starter for your conversations.

Hannah Brencher, author of *Come Matter Here* and *If You Find This Letter*

YOUR MESS MATTERS

YOUR MESS MATTERS

LUKE LEZON

Trusting the God Who Creates from Dust and Redeems by Blood

ZONDERVAN®

ZONDERVAN

Your Mess Matters

Requests for information should be addressed to:
Zondervan, *3900 Sparks Dr. SE, Grand Rapids, Michigan 49546*

ISBN 978-0-310-35571-7 (softcover)

ISBN 978-0-310-35574-8 (audio)

ISBN 978-0-310-35573-1 (ebook)

Cover design: Curt Diepenhorst
Cover illustration: © Shawn Hempel/Shutterstock
Interior design: Denise Froehlich

Printed in the United States of America

---

19 20 21 22 23 LSC 10 9 8 7 6 5 4 3 2 1

For my beautiful bride, Linds,
who saw my mess and loved
me enough to say "I do"

For my brother, Alex,
who knows every bit of this mess
and still loves the most

For my dad and mom, Jon and Tonja,
who made this mess and had no choice
but to love it. Being your son is one of
the great joys and gifts of this life.

To fall in love with God is the greatest romance; to seek him the greatest adventure; to find him, the greatest human achievement.

—Augustine of Hippo

Contents

My Darkest Hour

"I'm scared."

She pulled out her phone, hit send, and waited. Lindsey, my wife, stared at the chipped, white door, waiting for the cavalry to arrive. The man I had always been wasn't there. She had no idea who this was; I can't say I did either. There I sat as a stranger in my own home, not on a couch or a chair like a normal person would, but as a heap on the floor of our kitchen, staring blankly at our hideously cheap, brown, 1970s-looking cabinets in front of me. I could feel her glance at me, then at the door, then back at me once more.

It didn't take long. The door burst open.

I don't really remember everything about that day. How could it take doctors this long to figure out what's wrong with me? It had been months. How do they not know? What started out as a conversation with my wife turned into a screaming match that I won, but really, I lost. I yelled and paced; I cursed God. Lindsey kept telling me to calm down, but to no avail. Eventually, she gave up and cried on the couch because I was so far gone. Blackout fear, rage, and stress had taken over my mind. I collapsed on the kitchen floor and gathered myself into a sitting position, my chin resting on my knees. I felt frail, vulnerable, and exposed. Fear and stress had been bubbling up within me, and it had boiled over and burned my wife.

My dad, mom, and brother all filed through the door on the heels of one another. Cool, calm, and steady. They didn't say a word. My mom made a beeline for Lindsey and hugged her. My dad escorted them to the car. I heard Alex, my brother, ask Lindsey, "Where is he?"

The Talk

He walked into the kitchen and sat across from me in the same position I was in. He smiled. I couldn't keep the muscles in my face from pulling at the corners of my mouth ever so slightly, despite the circumstances. Different people have different assignments in your life. My parents are the best you could ever ask for, my wife is the love of my life and partner in everything, but if anyone needs to talk me off a ledge or speak sense into my life, they call Alex. After all, a brother is born for adversity.

"How's your day been?" he asked. I laughed, then we both laughed.

"Can't complain."

"What's going on inside your head?" The time for witty remarks and laughter was short-lived. I played his question over and over in my mind. I felt as if I didn't have anyone's attention up to this point. The doctors didn't seem to care. My family was certainly concerned, but not as concerned as I had been, not in front of me anyway. But recently things had felt as though I went from flying over the open ocean to accelerating into a nosedive at a breakneck pace. I was losing heart as rapidly as I was losing weight. The bloodwork couldn't rule out worst-case scenarios; we were getting ready for the possibility of having to schedule procedures. *Procedures.* Are you kidding me? I was twenty-four years old. Was this seriously happening to me? This kind of thing happened to other people, not to me. I had talked to people going through these situations, but I had never endured them myself.

"I'm tired. Weak. Scared. Stressed. Nobody knows what's wrong with me. It has been months. Months, plural. With an *s*. I don't know what else to do." I answered as plainly as I could. Alex didn't rush to answer. He's a man of few words, but each word is calculated, carefully thought out, and placed with purpose.

"There is nothing you can do."

"You should really look into motivational speaking." I couldn't help the passive-aggressive sarcasm from slipping through my lips. His words weren't exactly comforting.

He chuckled. "I'm serious. There is nothing you can do. The doctors are trying to figure this out, but it takes time. You have people around you who aren't going anywhere. You have Lindsey; you have us; but there is nothing you can do. If it's bad, we will endure the bad together. If it's good, we will celebrate. Either way, this mess is not intimidating God, and we aren't going anywhere."

I clapped back swiftly, annoyed that he wasn't freaking out in the middle of the storm with me, "It is a mess, isn't it?"

That's my clearest memory of the day. I do remember the rest of my family coming back into the living room at some point. Lindsey had to go to work. She was reluctant to do so, but what do you do? Call into work and say you have a DEFCON 1 situation at home and you don't know when you can come in? "Hello, my psychotic husband is screaming, pacing, falling down, sitting up, losing his mind like a scared child during a temper tantrum. I'll be there when we can find his pacifier." But the rest of the family assured her things would be fine. They brought me to their house, walked me to an empty bed, and I drifted off to sleep.

I Could Never, and I Will Never

I felt the edge of the bed dip slightly. Still exhausted from the events that had transpired earlier, I didn't even try to get up. I had no idea what time it was, but I must have been sleeping for a while because when I turned over, my wife was smiling down at me. She had come over after her shift ended and sat there scratching my back, not saying a word.

It's hard to say what I felt in that moment. It's even harder than trying to explain what happened during my emotional breakdown earlier in the day. I was embarrassed by the things I had said to her, yelled at her. I had screamed at her at the top of my lungs, told her that she didn't understand what I was going through. That she didn't care. That she was doing a poor job of helping me through my darkest hour. None of what I said could be further from the truth, but hurt people hurt people. It was shameful. Not because she shamed me, but because my own sin had affected not only me but the person I love more than anyone else in this world, more than myself.

She laid her head by mine, but I was turned away from her.

It hurts to look at someone you've hurt. She said, "Luke, look at me."

Reluctantly, I faced her. "How was work?"

"It was fine." She smiled. "Really slow, but it was fine."

"So, do you want to divorce me now, or what?" I figured I'd try to rule out the worst-case scenario right then and there. As long as the doctors were uncertain of what was going on with my health, I might as well try and find out what Lindsey thought was going on with our marriage after the day's events.

She laughed. "Nope."

"Well, good. This has been the highlight of my day." The shame hurt too much to keep looking at her, so I turned my back to her again. Not all pain is created equal.

She kissed me on the temple and whispered in my ear, "I could never, and I will never." She walked out and shut the door behind her.

Into the Mess We Go

I haven't told that story to many people; you are one of the first. I'd be lying to you if I said that was easy to write. It's embarrassing to think back on it and put it to paper. Who wants to recall their darkest hours? Let alone share them with others. I wish I could say that was the only messy situation I've experienced in my life, but it's just one of many. I'm sure you have plenty of messy stories of your own that are devastating to talk about or think about, but messes don't go away unless they're addressed. I shared one of my messiest moments with you before we begin this journey together because I want you to know that I'll be honest with you and remind you that you are not alone.

I don't personally know you. Yes, you, holding this book in your hands. I don't know everything about you. I don't know where you work, where you live, how much money you make, what your relationship status is, or what the messes in your life look like, but I do know this—your life is messy; my life is messy. But the central tenet that applies to everyone who reads this is that, whether you know it or not, Jesus Christ left the comforts of heaven to meet you in your mess, wash you clean, and bring you into the family as a child of God.

I have heard on multiple occasions that "God meets us in our mess." That sounds nice, doesn't it? But what does that really mean? Isn't God pristine and perfect?

When God made man, Genesis tells us that He formed him from the dust and breathed the breath of life into his nostrils. When God sent His Son, Jesus Christ, He lived anything but our idea of a perfect life. Yes, Jesus lived a perfect, sinless life, but He wasn't afforded the kingly comforts you would expect kings to enjoy. He didn't rule from a palace; He was homeless. He had no servants fanning His face with palm branches; He had followers lay them at His feet as He rode into Jerusalem one last time. He didn't wear a crown of jewels but a crown of thorns. He didn't sit on an ornate throne; He was nailed to an old rugged cross. He didn't ask others to spill their blood to protect His Kingdom; He poured out His own blood to bring us into His.

God doesn't work around the messes in your life; He works in them. It is by dust that we came into being and by blood that we came into receiving everything we will ever need in Jesus Christ. God doesn't just play in the dust; He pours out the blood. Messy work is divine work, and I am praying and believing that God is going to use this book as a resource to do divine work in you.

CHAPTER 1

Made in the Mess

I remember how fast it was spinning, the water gliding off my fingertips as the slimy texture whipped through my hands. I remember feeling as if I were in total control and yet that I had no control at all. It was exhilarating and terrifying.

My kindergarten teacher hovered over my right shoulder as I played god with my clay creation. She kneeled and spoke softly, trying not to distract the other gods in the room from their clay creations. "It looks like you're getting the hang of it."

My gaze shifted to the kid-sized potter's wheel in front of me. The lump of clay I had started with seemed slightly more formed than fifteen minutes ago, but not much. I wanted to make my mom a new coffee mug. I had been looking forward to this all week so that I could surprise her, but so far it looked like I was trying to make her a clay pancake. "Thanks, Mrs. Tuttle," I responded.

She pulled a pen out from behind her ear, taking notes as if she was getting ready to move on to the next god, but she picked up on my disappointment. "What's wrong, Luke?" She seemed genuinely concerned. I didn't see any harm in being honest.

"All I've done is make a mess. Look at this . . . this . . . thing . . ."

She searched my expression for the right words of encouragement, clicking her pen at a ferocious pace as she mulled over her words carefully. "I don't expect elementary art projects to be perfect, Luke. This is about having fun! Your mom is going to love whatever you make. I promise." She put her hand on my shoulder as if that would be enough to console the perfectionist in me. One thing elementary-age perfectionists do not want to hear is: "It doesn't have to be perfect." If Michelangelo wouldn't fall on his face in tears over the mere sight of my work, then it wasn't good enough.

"I know she'll like it. She has to. She's my mom. I just want it to be perfect. It's a mess right now." The other students started looking at us, thinking I was in trouble because of how long our conversation had carried on while they all spun their creations and laughed. Mrs. Tuttle caught on to this as well. She stood up, looked down at me, and said, "Luke, without the mess, there is no message. Your mom is going to love what this message means. I promise! Keep working on it; you're doing great."

I watched her scurry over to the neighboring tables, still feverishly clicking her pen. My classmates seemed to be enjoying the pottery lesson much more than I was. I thought, "Yeah, but without me, there is no mess."

That statement from a younger me packed a lot more truth than I realized. Mrs. Tuttle's comments were true as well. That wouldn't be the last time I heard the words "Without the mess, there is no message." I'm sure you've heard that saying, but if you peel back the layers, you find that without "me," there is no "(me)ss." Messes are chapters in life; they're a part of your story, but they aren't the point of your story. There is nearly unsearchable depth to the human soul. Only Jesus can reach our darkest corners, shine light on them, and beckon to us as we try to hide ourselves in them. He promises us a better way, The Way. Every person we come into contact with has, is, or will be going through *something*. I may not know what that something is, but the good news is that Jesus left the glory of heaven to meet you in your mess, wash you clean, and call you His.

We don't like messy. We want our lives to appear as clean as possible. We live in a culture that values pretty lies over ugly truths. We fear that if people knew about the messiness in our lives, then we would always be associated with that mess, labeled by it.

Make Something of Me

I love the way The Message paraphrases Psalm 40:17:

> And me? I'm a mess. I'm nothing and have nothing:
> make something of me.
> You can do it; you've got what it takes—
> but God, don't put it off.

The psalmist looks at the potter's wheel between his legs and sees the clay as a representation of his own life, and the coffee mug that he had in mind is a flat clay pancake. "I'm a mess. Make something of me."

That's one of our greatest fears, isn't it? To look at our life and feel as though it is going to waste. We feel as though we have all the resources and materials around us to make a coffee mug, to do great things with the life we've been given, but we've merely smeared a clay pancake on the canvas of our lives, failing to do what God has called us to do. To see the mess that is our lives and feel as though it cannot be salvaged is terrifying, but to salvage means to rescue. The bad news is that we cannot rescue ourselves. The good news is that we don't have to.

The psalmist writes to God because he knows that his mess requires God's intervention. He doesn't write to make something of himself. He writes to ask God to make something of him. He says to God, "I'm nothing and have nothing: make something of me." The beginning of God's greatest works in your life are realized when you've reached the end of yourself. If you are lost at sea but too proud to shoot off a flare, crying out for help, you will drown. But when you've reached the end of your pride and fire off the shot of surrender, you can be brought ashore to safety. Jesus invades your story on a mission to save. He not only meets you in your mess but thrives in it. He creates newness out of brokenness, life from death, something out of nothing. God is a doer of messy work, but it takes the proper perspective to see it.

Perspective for the Objective

Before the United States became the United States, we were a bunch of disgruntled neighbors with a common goal, which was to be a free nation. The problem was that we were up against one of the world's most powerful armies. They were highly-experienced, incredibly-disciplined, and well-funded.[1] We were none of those things.

The British had taken over Philadelphia, the capital at the time, a brutal winter was approaching, and it looked like the Americans were doomed to fail.[2] They needed help, and help arrived at Valley Forge on February 23, 1778, when ex-Prussian military captain Baron von Steuben stepped onto the scene to help Washington's troops.

He inspected the soldiers' housing, food, and equipment, and found their conditions to be such a mess that he commented, "No European army could have held together in such circumstances."[3] The National Parks Service even said that "what he [von Steuben] found was an army short of everything, except spirit."[4] He found out that the soldiers had all learned different drills and formations which created chaos on the battlefield. Von Steuben taught the troops how to quickly reload muskets, how to use a bayonet, and how to march as a unit in compact columns rather than long lines. He taught them methods that they had been missing, and when fighting began in the spring, the change in their methods was noticeable. Rather than getting crushed, the troops held their ground. Von Steuben had successfully molded a helpless army into a formidable force. His methods worked so well, in fact, that some of them are still used today.[5]

Before von Steuben showed up, the troops were getting crushed on the battlefield, the war wasn't going well for them. Have you ever felt that in your own life? Like God called you, but you're questioning it because it isn't going how you thought it would? The troops knew their calling was to fight for freedom, but the fight wasn't going well! Why? It's not that they lacked methods, but that they were given the *wrong* methods. When Baron von Steuben introduced the right methods to the madness, they were molded into who they were called to be to carry out what they were called to do.

Wrong methods create confusion, and if we're not careful, we'll think we're following the right method. But on the battlefield of life, it'll be chaos. God has a method of molding us into who He created us to be and what He has created us to do, but it can be really, *really* frustrating sometimes, can't it? We ask, "Lord, why do doors look open and then slam in my face? Why don't I have the opportunity they have? Where is the money? Why, Lord? Why? When? Hurry!" I believe God wants to do something special in and through you for His glory, but His process of preparation, His method of molding us, more often than not, is different from what we want and what culture sells us as success. We have to abandon a worldly perception of progress and grab hold of a godly perspective of progress.

Baron von Steuben's story is a story of perspective. He walked into a mess of a situation. He was working with an army that was hungry, had poor equipment, terrible housing, and that lacked the discipline to march together. That's how they were described, that's what the rest of the world saw, but he didn't simply see what everyone else saw. He peered beyond the mess. He saw a group that had grit and was willing to be made into something special, so he reworked them into a finely tuned vessel.

Get on the Wheel

We have to get on the wheel, not as the potter, but as the clay. In Jeremiah 18:2–6 (ESV), God says to Jeremiah,

> "Arise, and go down to the potter's house, and there I will let you hear my words." So I went down to the potter's house, and there he was working at his wheel. And the vessel he was making of clay was spoiled in the potter's hand, and he reworked it into another vessel, as it seemed good to the potter to do. Then the word of the LORD came to me: "O house of Israel, can I not do with you as this potter has done? declares the LORD. Behold, like the clay in the potter's hand, so are you in my hand, O house of Israel."

When Jeremiah goes down to the potter's house, he sees in verse 4, "the vessel of clay was spoiled in the potter's hand, and the potter reworked it into another vessel, as it seemed good to the potter to do." And He *reworked* it, as it seemed good to the *potter* to do. If you aren't in public, feel free to shout amen or at least write it in the margins if you know that what the Potter wants to do and what the clay feels like doing don't always line up. Sometimes God gives us what we need rather than what we want because what we want will move us toward our desires, but what we need will lead us toward our destiny. If a potter can take clay and turn it into different tools to help fulfill their purpose around a home, how much more do you think God will do in our lives if we keep a godly perspective as He works in the messiness of our lives?

Perspective is a powerful thing. If we would just tweak our perspective a little bit, we would change the trajectory of our path. To quote the great theologian Albus Dumbledore, "It is our choices that show what we truly are, far more than our abilities."[6] Von Steuben chose to help the American troops when they lacked equipment, nutrition, and direction. The troops chose to be obedient even though they were freezing, starving, and a severe underdog. Jeremiah sees the potter working at his wheel and even though the clay didn't turn out great the first time, the potter didn't throw the clay away, he reworked it. Will we tweak our mindset to adopt a godly perspective in the middle of life's uncomfortable moments of molding? Will we choose to be obedient and let God rework us as He sees fit? It's easy to say, but difficult to do.

Much like the situation von Steuben walked into, life is often at its messiest before we are finally able see our lives from a godly perspective. It's only after we've gotten through pain where we thought breakthrough wasn't possible, or after we've gone through that abysmal relationship or addiction that we may get a glimpse into what God was doing. Søren Kierkegaard said it best: "Life must be lived forwards, but can only be understood backwards."[7] We have to move forward with God through the mess to get to the other side, then we can look back and see what God saw.

I'm sure you've heard the saying "perception is reality," meaning that what people perceive is generally what they believe based on what they can see, hear, taste, touch, and smell, regardless of whether it's the truth. It means you're taking something at face value, believing that what's in front of you—and everything you can infer from that—is the truth, but there's always more than what meets the eye. A godly perspective doesn't bow to worldly perception.

Not long ago I thought I might have a cold, and as the days progressed, I didn't feel much better. I had been running a fever—nothing major but enough to take note. My throat had begun to hurt, and my body ached more on day three than it had on day one. Rather than going to see a doctor, I decided I would take matters into my own hands. I decided to do something I regret deeply. Listen to me: never, ever do this.

I googled my symptoms and ended up on WebMD. Unbeknownst to me, this was a catastrophic decision. WebMD is of the enemy. It is worldly perception at its absolute finest. Within twenty minutes I went from, "Advil ought to do it," to picking out my favorite wood-grain casket and a nice quote for my tombstone.

We're a lot like WebMD. When we see the messes in our lives, we try to make a diagnosis based on what we see. Godly perspective sees through the symptoms of the mess and looks ahead to what's to come. WebMD can give me their take at face value, but they don't have the final say.

Get off the Wheel

We have to get on the wheel as the clay, but that means we have to stop trying to play the part of the Potter. A godly perspective is one that looks at life through the lens of the faith and hope that we have in Jesus Christ. It takes 2 Corinthians 5:7 (CSB), "For we walk by faith, not by sight," from being the verse on your favorite throw pillow to the pillow you can sleep easy on at night no matter what your circumstances are. If I believe everything that I see to be certain, then I'm not looking at life through a proper Jesus-centered, cross-shaped perspective. I'm seeing the crucifixion of Jesus and failing to stick around for the resurrection of Jesus. It's a three-days-later mindset—seeing death through the perspective of resurrection. Certainty in the things we can see looks at our mess and says, "There is no hope.

This is just how things are." But a godly perspective doesn't discount the messes in our lives or sweep them under the rug. It brings them to the forefront, addresses them, and shines light on the darkness. Godly perspective helps us to have faith during the mess and see Jesus through it.

God gives Jeremiah a message that is directed toward the nation of Israel, using the illustration of the potter and the clay. Since God uses this illustration to speak to an entire nation, then He is certainly able use it to speak to us individually. But why choose a potter and clay? God could have simply told Jeremiah the point He was trying to make. Even if He didn't want to tell Jeremiah directly, He still has an infinite number of ways to get His point across, but He specifically chooses the potter and clay. Why? At this particular time in history, people were more familiar with the pottery process than we are today, but still, He could have chosen a handful of other illustrations. God is showing Jeremiah the messy work that goes into making pottery, and He's giving Jeremiah a powerful perspective on the way He works in the messiness of our lives.

In Jeremiah 18:6, where it says, "O house of Israel," write your name above it in your Bible. Put this book down, go get your Bible, and do it, or just write your name in the blank of this next sentence and read it to yourself. God says, "_______, can I not do with you as this potter has done? . . . Like the clay in the potter's hand, so are you in my hand" (ESV). Do you see that? God gives us the perspective we need to understand the illustration. We have a role. God is the potter. We are the clay.

In my elementary art class, I looked at the clay on the potter's wheel with great disappointment. The psalmist looks at the potter's wheel between his legs in Psalm 40 and sees the clay as a representation of his own life. He realizes that he doesn't need to be molding, he needs to be molded. He cries out, "Make something of me!" Often the greatest obstacle in our mess is ourselves. Rather than embracing our role as the clay, we try to play the potter, and we hate what we see because the wheel isn't ours; it belongs to the Potter.

Clay's purpose is maximized when placed in the hands of the potter, the same way that our lives are maximized when we place it in the hands of the God who gave us life in the first place, but it's not always comfortable. You can't just bring clay in from outside and start turning it into jars. I don't know if you've ever watched a potter turn a slab of clay into a jar, but it's messy and tedious. It is a process to create a functional piece with purpose. Clay can't be taken from the ground and immediately turned into jars. It has impurities that must be refined first. The clay is thrown on the potter's wheel, and water is applied to shape it. The clay gets pressed together, pulled apart, smashed down, built up, and when you think it's almost done, the finer details of the work begin. The lip is made thicker and wider so it will be stronger. The inside is stretched so it can hold more liquid or grain. The handle is shaped, made perfectly for a hand to hold on to it and carry the weight of its contents.

As the Potter works the clay, it has moments where it starts to form awkwardly or in a way that is contrary to what the Potter is creating it to thrive as, so He reworks it and reworks it some more. He doesn't toss it away and say, "That one was a bad piece. Thank you. Next!" No, He patiently works it into form. Finally, it must be put into a kiln to go through fire so that it will be sturdy enough to carry out the purpose for which is was created. It has to be submitted into the Potter's hands for it be worked and reworked again and again. As God molds and shapes you, it may look messy, but messy hands make beautiful pottery. There is beauty in it, and there is purpose in the process.

The Beauty of Broken Pieces

I met with a friend of mine at a local coffee shop the other day, and he asked me what I was writing about. I told him my thoughts on Jeremiah 18. I went through everything that I'd written up to this point, and as I talked, he said nothing. He didn't even make eye contact with me. He was hardly present, staring off into space while I rambled on. After I finished explaining what I had been writing, I still didn't get a response from him. It was as if he were sleeping with his eyes open. I fiddled with my coffee cup for an uncomfortable amount of time before finally deciding to be a little more direct. I snapped my fingers in his face and sarcastically said, "Hello? You there? Do you have any thoughts on that? Do you not like the idea? You can give me your honest thoughts. It won't hurt my feelings."

He looked up at me for the first time since we'd started talking. It was his turn to do the awkward fiddling with his coffee cup. He paused for a moment, then he pushed his cup to the side, folded his hands, and choking back tears, said, "I think it's great, man. I just can't help but hear what you're saying and think about my own life. I feel like my purpose and the piece I used to be is dysfunctional. I feel broken, like I was being used and was fulfilling God's purposes in my life, but somewhere along the way I fell apart. I broke."

If I took all of us and put our thoughts on a projector, we'd probably find that for each of us, somewhere on our journey, there is that thing or things we could point to and say, "*That* right there is the mess I'm afraid not even God could clean up or want to get near. That's where I began to believe I was too broken to be used. The shame and wounds from *that* moment. That's where my purpose was shattered." Whether that was abuse in your life, an addiction, dreams that never came to fruition, you lost someone that you were close to, your trust was betrayed by someone you thought would never hurt you, insecurity kept you from being who you felt called to be, but God brings true beauty and breakthrough through the broken pieces we never thought could come together again.

A few years ago, I read an article about the Japanese art of Kintsugi. Kintsugi is an art that repairs broken ceramics or pottery with a lacquer that has been mixed with gold, silver, or platinum. The idea behind it is that rather than hiding the damage that has been done to the piece, you magnify the beauty of the repairs that restored it. Even better, the repairs actually make the piece more beautiful and valuable than it was prior to being broken. Kintsugi is an art of perspective. Rather than seeing a bunch of broken pieces that need to be thrown away, you look at what once was and realize that what is to come is even more beautiful. You don't take the broken pieces, throw them together, seal them with a gold lacquer and say, "Look! It's as good as new!" No, you carefully pick up each piece and though it may take a while, you gently put each fragment back into its original place to help the piece serve its purpose, then you seal it with a beautiful, expensive lacquer, and say, "There it is, more beautiful than ever before." That's a godly perspective in a messy situation. It's a reminder of the beauty of being made new and whole through the redeeming work of Jesus Christ on the cross. No matter how broken we've been in our lives, no matter how bad that person hurt us, or what they said about us, no matter what we've done or what was done to us, Jesus Christ came down to this earth, picked up all our pieces, and sealed us with the lacquer of His blood that He willingly poured out for you and for me on the cross.

Somewhere in your story, maybe the shame you felt from a failed marriage kept you from feeling as though God could use you. Maybe someone convinced you to put your identity in what people think of you rather than what God says about you, and you feel like a prisoner to people's opinions, even though God has set you free. Maybe the deep emotional wounds from infertility have made you hopeless and you're worried that God is done with you. Or you've sought job opportunities and gone to all the interviews, but the fruitless job hunts continue as you fear for your financial security. Maybe you believe you're unlovable because you've never had a relationship that lasts, even though God calls you His beloved. Whatever it is for you, these perceptions hold no weight when it comes to an eternal perspective. You see the messes in your life and don't see anything that could clean things up. How can you clean up this mess? You can't, but Jesus can, and He has. You can shift your perspective, let the Potter have His wheel again. Surrender the messiness of your life into His hands. Our messes don't define us, they refine us.

Jeremiah isn't the only one who uses the illustration of the potter and clay. Isaiah 64:8 says, "You, Lord, are our Father. We are the clay and You are the potter; we are all the work of your hand." You are the work of His hand, the creation of the Creator. It's not always easy to surrender to God and let Him have His way in your life. I'm not here to try and convince you that it is. It's not always fun to say, "Lord, I am the clay and You are the Potter, Your will be done." I don't imagine that as Jesus agonized in prayer to the point of sweating blood in Gethsemane that He was particularly excited about submitting to the hands of the Potter. In fact, Jesus asks that this cup would pass from Him the night before His crucifixion, but that didn't stop Him from walking in obedience.

I don't want to tell you why you need to be confident in letting God have His way in your life. I want to journey with you and have a conversation about it, but allow me to at least tell you why I feel both confident and comfortable letting God have His way in my life. My God has skin in the game. He speaks to me in prayer and through His Word, but I can also look to Jesus and know that my God doesn't just talk the talk; He walked the walk. When I see Jesus, I know that my God isn't just a metaphysical idea. He died a brutally physical death to pay the penalty that I could not, by dying the death I deserved. My God doesn't look at my mess and tell me to get my act together. He extends grace by faith in His Son, Jesus Christ, and tells me that He has come to clean up my mess. Can I tell you something about the Lord's hands? About your Father's hands? The reason I'm confident and why I trust my life in His hands is that the hands that are doing the uncomfortable molding and shaping in our lives are the same hands that were stretched out on the cross to bring us eternal life.

Life is messy. The gospel is messy. I know you've been hurting. I know you've felt broken. I know you're stressed. I know you're busy with your studies. I know you've got a job, a budget, kids, and a spouse. I know you feel as though you're a poor mom or an underachieving husband. I know you want to grow with the Lord and in other areas of your life. I know you've felt less than. More importantly, He knows. Jesus knows our lives are messy. He didn't come for the healthy but for the sick. He came to call sinners to repentance, that we may be healed by His wounds. His body was broken so that we would be made whole. His blood was poured out so that we would have life in Him. He's never been afraid of a mess, and He won't be afraid of yours.

CHAPTER 2

The Soil You Despise

I remember going to the circus when I was growing up. Yes, an actual circus. I'm not sure if that's what the kids are doing for fun these days, but this was a *The Greatest Showman*–style circus: animals jumping through flaming hoops, people walking across tightropes, trapeze artists swinging from the rafters, dancers being shot out of cannons, and all that, except Hugh Jackman wasn't there, and Zac Efron didn't show up. The show was mesmerizing. Watching these people perform was nothing short of mind-blowing, but of all the acts, nothing grabbed the attention of the audience quite like the elephants. When the elephants walked into the room, everybody focused on them. You couldn't ignore them if you tried. The sheer size of them under a relatively small tent was frightening. Forget that there were humans surfing on their backs. The mere sight of these creatures boggled the mind because they were so large that they demanded we address them. There was literally an elephant in the room, and that brought a lot of clarity to an old saying.

Most of us have probably encountered an elephant in the room of our faith. But the difference is that rather than being transfixed on the elephant in the room—this massive, larger-than-life, impossible-to-miss, mind-numbing reality in our midst—we have trained ourselves to suppress the idea that it's there, because addressing it seems like a task that is larger than the elephant itself. I've often found that within Christian circles specifically, some of the most difficult truths to deal with are the ones people are afraid to acknowledge, even if they're in the room with us.

Operation Desperation

If God is so great, if He loves me so much, if I am His child and He wants the best for me, then why hasn't He cleaned up this mess in my life that I've been praying and pleading with Him to take care of? Why are there things in our lives that we cannot stand about ourselves, but struggle to get a handle on? Why doesn't God simply sprinkle some sort of miracle cleaner that gets rid of the stain on the surface and also kills the root of my struggle?

No matter where we're at in life, regardless of age, profession, or proclivities, the reality is that the thing we were struggling with yesterday didn't vanish today. The thing we have had to suffer through for as long as we can remember didn't go away when we prayed for God to take it away. The mess that clouds our minds and wreaks havoc in our lives didn't suddenly disappear or get swept under the rug. It is still prevalent, and it is still disrupting the flow of our lives, our relationships with our friends, family, and even our relationship with God. Even though we agonize in prayer over our problems, God hasn't made them go away, at least not yet. You still struggle with that irrational fear in your life, to keep your lustful desires in check, that merry-go-round of financial disappointment, those issues with your father, your battle with insecurity, your marital bouts that seem to leave you both exhausted and uninterested. You're still out of a job or still don't have a diagnosis. When the problem doesn't go away, you try to put it out of your mind, but you can't. You feel as though every time you bring it up to God, He must block your number or ignore your text about this specific issue, because He doesn't seem too keen on addressing the elephant in the room. You are trying to cultivate a life that looks like a garden full of life, but you feel as if you are stuck in soil that fails to produce the life you'd like to see.

At some point we end up answering our own questions, since we feel as though God is avoiding them, and we typically end up in one of two camps. The first camp is the camp of achieving. We think the messiness in our life is a result of not living our life well enough for God, and because of how short we have fallen, we're stuck in a mess. We believe that because of what we've done or haven't done, God is letting us sulk in our mess because that's what we deserve. We determine God's involvement or lack of involvement in our life on the basis of our achievements rather than His.

The second camp is the camp of deceiving. Our feelings deceive us by twisting the narrative of God's goodness and grace. We think that maybe God isn't as great as everyone else thinks He is and that we've deceived ourselves into believing that God actually cares for us. But really He's not that great of a

Father, and because of His neglect, we're stuck in our mess. We determine God's character and love for us on the basis of how we feel in the moment rather than who He has always been. Both are natural human conclusions, but both are also wrong.

Much of the misunderstanding in our relationship with God isn't a result of miscommunication but a lack of communication. God is always speaking to us through His Word, but are we willing to listen? Our minds get so focused on the soil we despise that we end up missing the miraculous work God can do in that very soil. Messes are miracle-making fertilizer. Don't focus so much on the mess that you miss the miracle.

In Exodus 14 the Israelites are in the middle of making their mass exodus from Egypt when the Lord tells Moses to have everyone camp at Pi Hahiroth, facing the sea. As Pharaoh and the army of Egyptians draw near, they charge toward the Israelites, who are understandably terrified. Scripture tells us in Exodus 14:10–12 that the people cry out to the Lord and say to Moses, "Was it because there were no graves in Egypt that you brought us to the desert to die? What have you done by bringing us out of Egypt? Didn't we say to you in Egypt: 'Leave us alone; let us serve the Egyptians'?"

The Israelites are letting both God and Moses know that they are not thrilled with the soil they find themselves in. This is a mess that appears to have catastrophic consequences. They are surrounded by opposition. On one side the Egyptians are pursuing them, and on the other is the sea, an obstacle too great to overcome. It has them stuck in soil that may as well be sinking sand.

But opposition isn't always an obstacle. Sometimes it's an opportunity. God had told Moses, "I will harden Pharaoh's heart, and he will pursue them. But I will gain glory for myself through Pharaoh and all his army, and the Egyptians will know that I am the LORD" (Exodus 14:4). The soil we find ourselves in often feels like an obstacle to overcome, but what if it is an opportunity to be overwhelmed by the glory of God? As the Egyptians are breathing down the neck of Israel, God splits the sea. What was seen as an obstacle became the door of deliverance for God's people. We can't stop walking with God once we reach the edge of the sea. We have to walk with Him through it. The mess that the Israelites were so focused on turned out to be the exact thing that God used to produce a miracle.

God rescued the Israelites quickly, but why doesn't He always do that for you and me? Why isn't God cleaning up this mess in your life when you've been praying and pleading with Him to do so? There is purpose in it. God's own Son suffered. We are wasting our time if we get stuck in only asking, "Why am I suffering?" It's a natural question to ask. The Psalms are evidence of that fact, but don't get stuck there. Everyone suffers in their own way! If you study Christian tradition, you will find that all the disciples suffered and died brutal deaths except John. Realistically, most of us reading this will probably not be martyred, but struggle and suffering in this life is a promise (John 16:33). It is a matter of when, not if. But your mess has meaning.

Banks and Bargains

I remember going with my dad to set up a checking account for the first time. I was young, too young to work, but I would help mow the yard or do other things to earn twenty bucks here and there. Dad wanted to move the money I had earned into an account, partially so I could start learning how to manage money with a debit card, but mostly because he didn't trust me with cash. It was more convenient for him and for me, and I'm pretty sure he relished the opportunity to teach me a thing or two about money.

We walked through the doors of Wells Fargo and waited for an agent. I took in my surroundings, doing my best to act like an adult. A bank felt like a place where you needed to act like an adult. The agent called us into her office, and we took a seat. I sat up straight, shoes flat on the floor, chest out. I was ready.

"So, what are we doing here today?" She looked at me for an answer. I looked at my dad, but he opened his eyes wide and nodded toward the lady, indicating that this was a man-up moment.

I deepened my voice, "Uh, I'm here to open a checking account."

"Is this your first account with us?"

"Yes. Yes, it is." I was settling in. I could feel my chest hair growing.

"Fantastic, when is your birthday?"

She kept asking questions, and to my surprise, I had the answers. I was setting up an account. At. The. Bank. Sure, my friends might be playing basketball at the gym, but I didn't have time for such childish things. I had dry cleaning to pick up after this.

"Okay, great. You're all set, Mr. Lezon."

It was almost getting to be too much. Mr. Lezon? She was talking to me, not my dad. Me. I was running this show.

"Actually, there is one thing left." She swiveled back toward me. "We just need that one-hundred-dollar deposit and then you'll be good to go!"

I sat back in my chair and looked at my dad, eyes wide, pride shot. My chest hair was ripped off. I was slightly hunched over, feet no longer flat on the floor, legs swinging in midair, and in my squeaky, puberty-stricken voice I said, "Huh?" I had never seen that kind of money in my life! A hundred dollars? She may as well have asked me for a million. Not only did I not have that kind of money, but I couldn't even work my way toward it. The only way I could get my hands on that kind of money was by hoping against hope that my dad would come through. The price was so astronomically high that I couldn't pay it even though it was required. I couldn't cover my cost.

Dad smiled at me, trying not to laugh. He reached for his wallet, pulled out a hundred-dollar bill, handed it to her, and said, "Yes, I've got it right here."

I didn't have that kind of money, but my dad used that opportunity to show me that he had me covered. My pride swelled at that time, even as a kid, as though I had it all figured out. It wasn't until I came to the end of myself and my own abilities that I was able to see how in need I was and how good my dad was to reach out and take care of what I owed. Sometimes our Father brings us to seemingly impossible obstacles to reveal His immeasurable power and grace. We don't need more people who think they have it all figured out; we need more people who know they don't. We need to make our way out of the camps of achieving and deceiving and make our way into the camps of believing and receiving.

Romans 5:1–2 says, "Therefore, since we have been justified through faith, we have peace with God through our Lord Jesus Christ, through whom we have gained access by faith into this grace in which we now stand. And we boast in the hope of the glory of God." We can get caught up in thinking we aren't living our lives well enough or that God just doesn't care. But Romans reminds us that we achieve nothing by our own accomplishments, and we can't allow ourselves to be deceived into thinking that God isn't a good Father. We have to believe that God's perfect love for us was manifest and displayed in the person of His perfect Son, Jesus Christ, and receive the payment that Jesus made on our behalf. By the cross, our debt was paid. By the resurrection, that payment cleared. By grace through faith, our credit is perfect. The check cleared, our balance has been paid, and it has been paid in full for those who have repented and accepted Jesus. We are justified through the death, burial, and resurrection of Jesus.

If you're in Christ, this is your reality, even on your worst days, in the middle of your largest messes, and through the sufferings of your fiercest struggle. But what about the struggle? Why does the mess remain? Sure, Jesus made a way for me. Sure, maybe He does care about me, but what now? I'm still in this soil that I despise. Keep reading in Romans 5:3–4 (ESV), "Not only that, but we rejoice in our sufferings, knowing that suffering produces endurance, and endurance produces character, and character produces hope." What does that mean? It means it's time for us to embrace the smell of manure.

The Miracle of Manure

Dr. Carl Rosen is a professor and the head of the Department of Soil, Water, and Climate at the University of Minnesota in Saint Paul. In his biography on the University of Minnesota's website, Rosen says, "The responsibilities of my research and extension programs include identifying needs and establishing priorities in areas of plant nutrition and improving fertilizer use efficiency . . ."[1] Allow me to save you from death by boredom. Long story short, this guy is an expert in knowing how to grow stuff. He wrote an absolute thriller of an article with his colleague Peter M. Bierman, titled "Nutrient management for fruit and vegetable crop production: using manure and compost as nutrient sources for vegetable crops." In that article they say, "Manure is a *valuable* fertilizer for *any* farming operation and has been used for centuries to supply *needed* nutrients for crop growth." They continue to say, "Manure produced on or near a vegetable farm provide *many benefits* and should be beneficially utilized whenever possible," and finally, "proper use of manure and compost *is essential* from both a production and environmental standpoint" (italics added).[2]

I don't tell you all this because I thought you might enjoy a brief stroll through Manure and Compost 101. I'm telling you because your struggles and sufferings—the mess you find yourself in that you so desperately want to go away—isn't there because God ran out of hobbies and now He's creating messes in your life just to spice things up. Your mess, your crap situation, if you will, may be the soil that God is using to cultivate the crops you most desperately need. Maybe the soil you're in, which you believe is suffocating the garden of your life, is really helping sprout forth a crop that your garden needs in order to be all that God has created it to be. It's deepening the roots of your faith, helping you grow in ways that you wouldn't have otherwise. The crops I'm talking about aren't fruits and vegetables; they're crops that keep your faith alive in the middle of famine. I'm not talking about crops that will keep your physical body satisfied but crops that will nourish your soul and help feed your faith in Jesus, regardless of the season you find yourself in. God cultivates crops like faithfulness, endurance, righteousness, trust, and steadfastness in the soil we despise.

I'm sure you know the answer to this, but let me ask anyway. Do you know what the most popular flower is? Correct, the rose. Roses come in many colors, and they have many meanings depending on their color, but they are most symbolic as a tangible declaration of love. They're so hard not to love that you are almost guaranteed to see them at a wedding. Do you know what helps roses grow? You nailed it, manure. You don't have to take my word for it, though. Take Martha Stewart's. She describes the soil requirements on her rose growing guide like this: "Roses prefer a slightly acidic soil. To enrich your soil, use manure. Be generous in applying it; your roses will thank you."[3]

The soil you despise not only produces crops that feed your faith but brings forth beauty in ways you could have never imagined and in places you didn't think were possible. Don't despise the soil you're in. The trick to transformation is trials. God loves to garden in the soil of struggle. It's where He raises up some of His most satisfying, beautiful work, even though the process of gardening is messy.

The Struggle and the Blessing

Consider some of the following Bible passages.

> Endure hardship as discipline; God is treating you as his children. For what children are not disciplined by their

> father? If you are not disciplined—and everyone undergoes discipline—then you are not legitimate, not true sons and daughters at all. Moreover, we have all had human fathers who disciplined us and we respected them for it. How much more should we submit to the Father of spirits and live! They disciplined us for a little while as they thought best; but God disciplines us for our good, in order that we may share in his holiness. No discipline seems pleasant at the time, but painful. Later on, however, it produces a harvest of righteousness and peace for those who have been trained by it.
>
> HEBREWS 12:7–11

> In all this you greatly rejoice, though now for a little while you may have had to suffer grief in all kinds of trials. These have come so that the proven genuineness of your faith—of greater worth than gold, which perishes even though refined by fire—may result in praise, glory and honor.
>
> 1 PETER 1:6–7

> Count it pure joy, my brothers and sisters, whenever you face trials of many kinds, because you know that the testing of your faith produces perseverance.
>
> JAMES 1:2–3

Do you see a theme here? The struggles and sufferings of the mess you find yourself in may not feel ideal, but they are imperative for your faith to flourish because they help you produce crops that only come from extreme conditions. In Romans 5:3 (ESV), it starts off with "Not only that . . ." It reminds us that we have as much reason to rejoice on the mountaintop as we do in the valley, because no suffering we endure on this earth is greater than the glory set before us in Jesus.

I read a devotional the other morning that I've been reading for the better part of the last six years, and I came across a poem that said,

> Strange and difficult indeed
> We may find it,
> But the blessing that we need
> Is behind it.[4]

That is one of the most simplistic ways of bringing understanding to ugly, complex situations that I've been able to find. Most of the time we find ourselves sulking in our messes. We have a hard time seeing purpose in the messes of life, but there are always blessings behind them. God brings deliverance through the very soil we despise. It's not always in the form we want or expect it to be, but it's there. The blessing we're praying for is often found just beyond the struggle we're enduring.

Round Trip Ticket: From Eden to Gethsemane

When humanity fell, in the garden of Eden, Adam and Eve chose to disobey God and walk in their own ways rather than His. In that instant, sin, and the messiness that comes along with it, entered the world. As we move forward in time to a different garden, from Eden to Gethsemane, we see Jesus praying, sweating blood, pleading before the Father, asking Him to take His cup of suffering away. But it didn't happen. Jesus was arrested, tried, and crucified, but He was also raised. God worked in the soil of Jesus's suffering to cultivate the crops that humanity needed most—redemption and salvation.

Romans 5:12 says, "Just as sin entered the world through one man, and death through sin, and in this way death came to all people, because all sinned." But when we drop down just a few verses, we read in Romans 5:17: "If, by the trespass of one man, death reigned through that one man, how much more will those who receive God's abundant provision of grace and of the gift of righteousness reign in life through the one man, Jesus Christ!"

Adam and Eve walked in Eden with God, but they walked away from God in disobedience when they ate from the Tree of the Knowledge of Good and Evil. Jesus walked in Gethsemane praying to God, and He walked toward God in obedience when He said, "Father, if you are willing, take this cup from me; yet not my will, but yours be done" (Luke 22:42). The restoration of Eden began as Jesus planted the seed that would bring forth the tree of redemption, a seed that could only be cultivated in extreme conditions, in the messy soil of Jesus's suffering and by the blood of the cross.

God can garden in any soil you believe is toxic. Jesus was buried and planted in the tomb for three days. It looked as if nothing beautiful could come from the gruesome mess of the cross, but heaven simply waited on the edge of its seat. By His blood, and through the power of the resurrection, life sprouted forth from the soil of suffering in a way we never could have imagined: eternal life through the very alive King Jesus.

I don't know what you're facing as you read this, but I am certain of this: God's love never fails. You are loved with an everlasting love that cannot be blocked out by your sin and struggle. Love doesn't give up on you; it extends grace to you so that in your struggle, you can struggle well. That mess you're in will lead to growth in your relationship with God that you may never have seen without it. This isn't happening without purpose. This isn't going unnoticed by God. He sees it and uses it. He is molding your character and showing you His. Whatever mess you're in, whatever soil you despise, be encouraged: God is a doer of messy work.

CHAPTER 3

Lessons on Letting Go

I don't know about you, but I love structure as long as it isn't restricting. I love having a plan that facilitates creative freedom and challenges the way I think. I love waking up early and staying up late, investing in something I'm passionate about. If there is a foundation, I want to build on it. I think that's why I love sermons. The foundation is Christ, God's Word, and everything from there is an illustration, a story, and supporting verses that bring people back to that foundation. That's why this six-month stretch of an untraceable illness was so difficult. I wasn't standing where I needed to stand. The foundation I stood on had started to crack; the structure that used to be there was falling apart. Something was very, very wrong, but I was determined to downplay it.

Lindsey, my bride of less than one year, and I pulled out of our apartment parking lot before the sun could peek over the rolling hills of Fayetteville, Arkansas. Thankfully, Puritan Coffee Bar was awake before the rest of the world. We pulled up, got some miracle fluids, and headed south on I-49 toward Little Rock. From there we would hit Memphis, Birmingham, and finally Atlanta, Georgia, where I was slated to preach. I hadn't been feeling great for a few weeks, and finally I confessed to Linds.

"I don't know what is going on with me lately, but I haven't felt great."

"You don't look great, but maybe you're just tired?"

"You're right. Coffee will help."

I had traveled a lot lately: New York City, home, New York City, Israel, home, Grand Rapids, home, Atlanta, home, and now back to Atlanta. Maybe all that travel was catching up with me? I wasn't sure. Was all that travel an explanation for nausea, diarrhea, dehydration, and stomach aches that had me doubled over? I played doctor in the privacy of my own mind. Linds had *Grey's Anatomy* on often enough for me to feel like a qualified surgeon, but I hadn't determined a diagnosis.

The day of the event, I felt fine. I figured I must have had a virus that had ran its course. I just needed to be patient enough to give it time. I preached that night without feeling queasy, and the night went remarkably well. Linds and I took a few photos afterward and went back to the place where we were staying. We were exhausted, but my spirits were high. I thought I had finally turned the corner on whatever it was that I had been battling, but that peace didn't last long.

I got out of the shower and was about to lie down, but I saw that Lindsey sat up in bed, looking a little rigid. She must have been waiting for me to get out of the shower because she studied me for a moment, then looked at her phone, then at me, then once again at her phone. I raised an eyebrow.

"What?" I asked hesitantly. She was acting so strange.

"How much do you weigh?"

"I don't know. I've always weighed around 195. Why?"

"Look at these photos you were tagged in tonight."

She didn't need to say anything. I knew what she saw. It was obvious. My face looked sunken, my jawline more prominent, and not in a James Dean kind of way. I looked unhealthy, much thinner than I typically was. My skin was starch white; my eyes were dark around the edges. If I were missing a nose, I could have passed as a second cousin of Voldemort.

"Maybe it's just the angle the photo was taken at or som—" I didn't get an opportunity to finish my sentence. She yanked me by the arm and dragged me into the bathroom of the Airbnb we were staying at. She slid the scale in front of me and tried to push me on it. Reluctantly, I stepped on.

"How did we not notice this before?" Her voice was steady, but I could tell she was serious. I was down eighteen pounds, to 177. We got in the car and headed home, where we would end up in the emergency room.

The 1 in 60 Rule

Pilots have this rule they follow called the 1 in 60 rule. For every degree that you fly off course, you end up missing your mark by more than ninety feet per mile that you fly. So for every sixty miles that you fly, you will end up being off track by a mile or worse. My health had flown well over sixty miles, and it was well over one degree off course.

Sometimes we have a hard time diagnosing the things that are right in front of us because it's difficult to detect the small incremental changes. Lindsey and I see my body every day. We don't see massive changes day in and day out. The changes can go unnoticed, and by the time you realize you've been taking little steps in the wrong direction, you're headed east when you thought you were going west.

Any momentum I thought I had toward being healthy suddenly took a turn for the worst. The wind of positivity that had filled my sails earlier in the day plummeted. I quickly drifted into waters that I had yet to explore, waters that would take me to an island that only God and I could get to.

It's a lot easier to take a step when you can see what you're stepping toward. If we can't see the end of the path, we become weary of putting ourselves in a position that we're unfamiliar with, but messes don't ask to be made, they just are. Whether you love structure or tend to fly by the seat of your pants, you probably appreciate clarity as much as the next person. That's why this journey became so difficult. I didn't see it coming, and I couldn't see where it was going to end. Lindsey and I had to move in with my parents. I couldn't work, couldn't move. I had no clarity, no direction. It was the stuff of nightmares. I'll tell you the rest of the story, but I want to make sure we look at it through the lens of the gospel to help you navigate through your own story.

Letters from Prison

Paul writes a chunk of his New Testament letters from prison. They're known as the Prison Epistles—Ephesians, Philippians,

Colossians, and Philemon. Something about the uncertainty of Paul's situation makes these letters strike a chord in our own hearts. He's sitting in prison, trusting that God is using the mess he's in to move the message of God's kingdom forward. Meanwhile, questions have to be looming in Paul's mind, none more obvious than this one: will he make it out alive?

Paul writes the book of Philippians while under house arrest, but that doesn't detract from the joyfulness of his letter to the Philippians. Paul loves the Philippian church. His letter to them is probably the warmest of the New Testament, which isn't all that shocking. They were a pretty healthy congregation compared with many of the other churches Paul had planted, and they even supported him financially. As Paul is imprisoned, they send a member of their church, Epaphroditus, to take Paul a gift. Being incarcerated had serious social ramifications. Most people would have distanced themselves, but instead, the Philippians come near to Paul in his moment of need. Most of us probably haven't been to prison—maybe some of you have—but we all probably have our own version of prison. The messiness of life can cause us to feel shackled to uncertainty, and it creates confusion in our hearts. We worry when the finances are *still* tight, our marriage is *still* exhausting, our kids are *still* battling loneliness, our hearts are *still* healing from addiction or abuse. Have you ever felt that? Like you're trapped? As though you're walking through a thick fog without clarity or direction? I think most Christians would be willing to admit that one of the great frustrations of walking with God is that sometimes we don't have a clue why He has us traveling the path we find ourselves on. That's why Paul's letter to the Philippians is so challenging.

Philippians 4 is the tail end of the letter, but we also find ourselves at the beginning of an answer to questions we ask all the time. Why is the path that we're on unclear? How did I travel this far off course? A lot of times the messes in our lives aren't as bad as the emotions that they stir up inside us. That's what I faced with this illness. The messiness of it was terrifying, but the way it made me feel was worse. Being confused and scared gets old. We want to know why we have times when we lack direction in life, which makes us frustrated and confused. We'll get to that, but let's jump back into my story.

Rock Bottom

"Lukas Luhyayzon?" The nurse called my name, and Lindsey and I stood up.

"That's me."

"Did I pronounce your last name correctly?"

"It was close enough." If you have a strange last name, you know that every teacher you ever had butchered your last name, so at some point you just learn to go with it.

She took every test imaginable. Blood tests, swab tests, urine tests, even stool samples, which, by the way, can we talk about that for a second? Stool samples are up there for one of the most "you want me to do what?" moments of life. It's hard to look someone in the eye as they tell you to get your own poop in a bottle and then in full confidence walk a tube of poop to the counter and say, "Hey, just dropping a gift off for doctor so-and-so." They sent us home and scheduled a follow-up appointment with another doctor. In the meantime, though, I was still losing weight.

My appointment came, and they weighed me. 171.

Twenty-four pounds down, hopefully no more to go. I had never wanted to gain weight so badly in my entire existence. The doctor went over the results with us and said everything was normal. They scheduled me for a more in-depth blood test to cover all our bases. Nervously, I asked the doctor on our way out, "This isn't going to be a worst-case scenario or anything, is it? I don't have cancer, right?"

He looked at me and kind of chuckled, trying to put my mind at ease without lying. "We can't rule it out, but don't go there yet." He gave me a prescription for some of the most powerful antibiotics on the market and sent us downstairs for the advanced blood test. I hadn't received bad news, but it wasn't necessarily good news either. I wasn't given a cancer diagnosis, but there simply aren't adequate words to describe the deafening ringing in your ears that blocks out clear thinking when you ask the doctor if you could have cancer and they basically say "maybe."

The nurse finished drawing my blood. She took the needle out, the rubber band off, and handed me a Band-Aid. "You're good to go!"

"When will you get results? Will it tell us what is causing the weight loss?"

"We think, we hope that we'll know soon!" She gave me an unconvincing smile. All these exclamation points were not boosting my confidence.

We didn't know soon.

The results had come back normal. January turned to February, February turned to March, and still no answers. As a result, I had my infamous meltdown. During this waiting, the doctors wanted to take a thorough look at me from the inside out. I had a colonoscopy and an endoscopy, investigating both the attic and the basement. It had been almost four months of wondering if I had cancer. After the colonoscopy they were finally able to rule out cancer. It was a huge relief. My family sobbed, and I was thankful, but the doctors did make an interesting discovery. My white blood cell count, specifically my eosinophil white blood cell count, was through the roof in my guts. Eosinophils are typically associated with parasite activity. They didn't know what kind of parasite or how it got there, so they put me on a waitlist to see an infectious disease specialist.

It was late March, nearly April, and the mess lingered. The only hope I held on to was that the antibiotics were killing the parasite. Fortunately, my appointment with the infectious disease specialist was coming up, so I figured I should shower. I'd been so frail and weak that if I wasn't lying down, I was sleeping. But I mustered the strength to carry myself to the bathroom. I slipped my shirt over my head. I wasn't facing a mirror directly, but out of the corner of my eye I caught a glimpse of my shoulder blade protruding under my skin. I turned around to look closer, my back fully exposed to the mirror as I craned my head over my left shoulder. I was so thin that my shoulder blades looked like wings, as though I could have taken flight if I got a running start. I could count the vertebrae near the top of my spine, and as I began to pirouette and take inventory of my new, undesirable features, I saw my ribs clearly enough to measure the gap between each one. Out of curiosity I stepped on the scale. 155. Forty pounds down.

I stepped into the shower. The water was scalding hot, but I didn't care. I put my head against the wall and let the water pound against my back for so long that I could feel the skin turning raw. "What are You doing, God? Where are You?" I cried out loud. I hadn't been healthy since December. The doctors were pretty sure I had a parasite, but I wasn't getting any better. I didn't know what to do anymore, so right there in the shower, I started to worship. I fell down on my hands and knees, and I wept. Life had felt as clear as mud. I was pathetically weak, but right there in that moment, I felt God's loving arms grab hold of me in such a powerful way that I couldn't help but repent, asking Him to forgive me for the way I had reacted up to this point. All I wanted to know was exactly what the diagnosis was and how to clean up my mess. *At this point I didn't care what it would take to become healthy again, I was just tired of wandering through a fog.*

Confusion, Clarity, and Peace

Sometimes we react similarly when we find ourselves in a crisis of faith. When we are searching for clarity or direction in our lives, in any situation or circumstance, we often find ourselves frustrated and confused. We don't care what it takes, we just want God to give us answers. We would rather have God strike us with lighting from heaven that reveals His plan for us than walk around unstruck but confused. Because of human nature, we inherently allow confusion in our lives, which creates chaos. When we don't have clarity regarding the direction our life is headed, we come to this inevitable fork in the road of our faith. We can walk the road of panic or peace. I panicked. I handled this trial so poorly, but it took me a while to understand why. I kept asking God for clarity amid all the confusion, but clarity wasn't what I needed. In Philippians 4:4 (ESV) Paul says, "Rejoice in the Lord always; again I will say, rejoice." I hate that, don't you? Let's be real. The guy in chains is telling us to rejoice, not once but twice. How am I supposed to argue with that? He not only tells us twice to rejoice but tells us to rejoice always, even in the messiness of life. He goes on in verses 5–7: "Let your gentleness be evident to all. The Lord is near. Do not be anxious about anything, but in every situation, by prayer and petition, with thanksgiving, present your requests to God. And the peace of God, which transcends all understanding, will guard your hearts and your minds in Christ Jesus."

In our walk with God, we will find ourselves in seasons where life doesn't feel like we're walking down a straight path with a map in hand. It feels more like we're white-water rafting in a torrential downpour, through a fog, without a paddle, completely at the mercy of the current, and hitting every rock along the way. In our quest for clarity, we often take a wrong turn and end up panicking, but Paul gives us helpful directions in verses 4–6. He says,

1. Rejoice always.
2. Let your gentleness be known to everyone.
3. Don't be anxious about anything.
4. Pray about everything.
5. Petition (recognize His authority and respectfully ask of) God.
6. With thanksgiving present your requests to God.

Why give us all these directions? Because in verse 7 he tells us where that path leads, "And the peace of God, which transcends all understanding, will guard your hearts and your minds in Christ Jesus." In our quest for clarity, we are missing out on something so much greater—peace. Verses 4–6 aren't suggestions; they're commands. And verse 7 isn't a possibility; it's a promise. We will have moments in life where we feel lost and are unable to see the end of the road. I was in one of them, but when exercising the muscles of faith, there is no greater workout than embracing peace in the middle of the messiness of life. If you're lacking peace, ask yourself, Do I complain more than I rejoice? Do I have gentleness toward others or am I harsh with them? Am I riddled with anxiety, not regarding the necessity of care for mental health but because I choose to dwell on worst-case scenarios at the onset of every dilemma? Do I invest in prayer or borrow from worry? Am I prideful or humble in my requests of God?

As Paul sits under house arrest, uncertain of what will happen to him, he doesn't promise that God will give you clarity but that He will give you peace. In 1 Corinthians 14:33 (ESV), Paul is talking about spiritual gifts in the church, but the verse still applies to what we're talking about because it speaks to the character of God: "God is not a God of confusion but of peace." The antidote to your confusion in your walk with God isn't clarity in the mess, but peace in the mess. Better than the clarity of knowing where your path leads is the peace of knowing that God is with you every step of the journey, no matter where and no matter what. That is infinitely better than knowing what, when, where, and how your boat will float to shore in these unchartered waters. Infinitely better.

Friendly Fire

I finally got in to see the infectious disease specialist. He seemed like a determined guy; he wanted to get to the bottom of this as badly as I did. He asked me a few questions, then he asked if I was on any medications. I told him about the crazy antibiotics I had been taking for months. We ran more of the same tests that I'd done a million times, then he called me.

"Luke, you doing all right?"

"Yes, sir. Did you find anything else out?"

"Well, buddy. You have C. diff."

"I have what?"

"*Clostridioides difficile* infection."

Long story short, he told me that he wasn't entirely sure how I got it, but that I did have a parasite at one point. When the doctors saw how high my white blood cell count was, they gave me these super-powered antibiotics to kill the parasite, and they worked. But they worked too well. Antibiotics can cause C. diff. The antibiotics killed the parasite, but they also killed all the healthy bacteria in me. Our bodies are constantly at war, and mine had no defenses. As a result, I had contracted a new infection. C. diff is essentially really bad diarrhea. What the infectious disease doctor didn't know is that before he could tell us that I had C. diff, C. diff had made it clear that it had me.

You have to laugh in the messiness of life, or otherwise you will be miserable. Laughter is medicine for the soul. Proverbs 17:22 says, "A joyful heart is good medicine, but a broken spirit dries up the bones" (CSB). Laughter is like a well. Sometimes you get to your lowest moment and it's there that you find what you need. When the water touches your lips, when you're able to pull the laughter up from the deepest, darkest places in your life, you find the fuel you need to keep going. Sometimes you have to dig deep to get to the good stuff.

When I tell you that I had diarrhea during all this, it's not like the diarrhea after you eat a bad tuna roll. Niagara Falls couldn't compete with this. It was as if the Hoover Dam had cracked, and diarrhea rushed out of me. I could have been America's greatest source of hydroelectric power during this six-month span.

I woke up one night and checked my phone: 2:43 a.m. Lindsey was still asleep. I looked up at the ceiling and wondered why my legs felt wet and why our room smelled funky, so I walked to the bathroom. I turned the lights on and immediately found out that C. diff had turned the clock back twenty-two years. I had crapped the bed. Everywhere. At twenty-four years old. Sometimes guys will get together and ask each other if they've passed gas around the girl they're dating or thinking about proposing to. Sometimes I'll hear couples say how after they've had a child together, nothing freaks them out about each other anymore. Lindsey and I went ahead and skipped all those steps. Every. Single. One. There is no casual way to wake up your wife in the middle of the night and explain this situation, and yet, I had to try.

"Hey, babe. Get up."

"Huh? Why? What's going on?"

"I crapped the bed. It's everywhere. It's on me. It's on you. I think some might have even hit the ceiling somehow. It's a crap crime scene in here. It's bad. I don't know what's going on, but it's not good."

She looked up at me half-asleep and said, "Go shower."

"Say no more." She didn't have to convince me. By the time I got cleaned up, Lindsey had cleaned everything. The crappy (literally) sheets were in the washer, and she had laid down fresh new sheets. They were neatly folded, and there was a glass of cold water on my nightstand. She showered after I got out, then came back to bed. I couldn't sleep.

"Sorry to wake you up like that. It had just been a while since I'd done anything romantic for you. Side note—maybe we should just burn those sheets." I couldn't help but make a joke, but I quickly went back to feeling helpless. "I can't wait till this is over."

"Luke, it will end at some point. Your mess is my mess. Don't say sorry like there is anything you can do about it, but let's pray about it before you start freaking out again." I prayed quickly so that she could get back to sleep. After I finished praying, she scratched my back until I fell asleep.

I tell you this for two reasons. First, I want you know that it's not only okay, but it's encouraged that you laugh in the middle of the messiness. Second, because I want you to know that the journey isn't just about the mistakes you make and the milestones you cross; *it's about whom you cross them with.* Don't miss the opportunity to rejoice with thanksgiving to God for the people in your life that don't only love you in your mess but help you clean it up and say, "Your mess is my mess."

So, I'm sure you're wondering how I finally got healed. Getting rid of C. diff is extremely difficult. It was as hard to get rid of as the parasite was, and after having multiple infections in my body, I didn't care what it took to get healed, I was willing to do it. Let me tell you, God has a sense of humor.

The doctor went over my options. They all seemed to be a hopeful process. This "might work" or this "could help," but then he said, "There is one way that's a newer procedure, but it has been wildly successful at getting rid of C. diff. It's more of a mental hurdle than anything."

"Doctor, I don't care what it is. I'll do it. How long does it take to recover?"

"Studies show that you should be back to normal after the procedure."

"All right then, I'll do it. What is it?"

He looked at me cautiously and said, "Now, don't freak out when I tell you this. Just hear me out. The procedure is an FMT, a fecal microbiota transplant. The point of the fecal transplant is to get healthy bacteria back into your system. You have none. We have to get it from somebody else, and it has to be approved. So your wife or someone you know can't be the poop donor, it has to be someone that's been approved already, but that means we know that it will be effective. This will work, and I believe you will be healed immediately."

Are you sure you always want to know the details of the journey God has for you?

"Hold up. Hold on. Pump the brakes. Just . . . just wait a minute. We can't skip past what you just said like you didn't just say what you just said. What you're saying is that you want to do a procedure where you put someone else's poop inside me?"

"Yes, that's what I'm saying."

"Not someone I know?"

"Does it really matter? From what I know, it's a donor from Harvard, and the person has to be in good shape because obese individuals have different bacteria than those with a strong body mass index."

"Will this make me smarter and more ripped?" I had to ask.

"We can test that afterward." He laughed with me.

"Let's do it. Let's put someone else's poop in me. Can't wait."

You want to talk about a messy situation? It doesn't get

filthier than that. How ironic that one of the symptoms of my health crisis was actually going to be what healed me in the end. God works this way. He works so powerfully in the middle of our mess that He can take what we think is killing us and use it to strengthen us. I didn't get smarter or leaner, but I was healed, and that was good enough for me. My faith was tested in ways I had never imagined. It took six months to be healed, but more importantly, it took six months to understand the discipline of letting go of my desires. I needed to learn that I don't need to see the whole picture before I start the puzzle. I just needed to start working with the pieces I was given, to stay anchored to peace when nothing else was clear.

Keep Stepping

Philippians 4:8 says, "Finally, brothers and sisters, whatever is true, whatever is noble, whatever is right, whatever is pure, whatever is lovely, whatever is admirable—if anything is excellent or praiseworthy—think about such things." If you look back at verses 4 through 6, you'll remember that there were six directions that ultimately led to verse 7, which tells us that "the peace of God, which transcends all understanding, will guard your hearts and your minds in Christ Jesus." Now, in verse 8, we're given eight new directions: to think on whatever is

1. True
2. Noble
3. Right
4. Pure
5. Lovely

6. Admirable
7. Excellent
8. Praiseworthy

Why? Because it leads to this in verse 9: "Whatever you have learned or received or heard from me, or seen in me—put it into practice. And the God of peace will be with you." Peace—that is what we must seek. Clarity will come and go, but peace is always available in Christ. Paul tells us how to purge our lives of blockades to peace and gives us the tools to cultivate fertile ground in our hearts and minds, where peace can flourish. Verse 7 tells us that "the peace of God" is given to us, and verse 9 tells us that "the God of peace" will be with us. God not only gives you peace; He is peace. Many of us desire clarity because we want to know where God is leading us. If we can't see the end of the journey, we won't take the first step onto the path. Where He is taking us is important, but not nearly as important as the fact that He goes with us. That gives us the confidence to step toward whatever He has called us to.

Not Only If, Even If

Do we trust in our circumstances or in God? It's so much easier to give in to worry than it is to cling to Jesus. If I never went through this health mess, I would never have come out with renewed faith and trust that I didn't even know I needed. When we don't know what else to do, we can either worry or worship. Whether you're in the valley or on the mountaintop, be persistent in your praise. That's what changed my life. At my weakest moment, when I had no hope, no end in sight, in the shower I wept and I worshipped. Worshipping in the mess declares trust in the power of Jesus's victory on the cross over every battle that we're facing. God's glory shines the brightest when we worship through our pain and suffering, because even when we weep, we can rejoice and know that God is working all things together for our good and His glory. And not just the easy things, but *all* things. Don't be an only if believer; be an even if believer. He is good in the valley, on the mountaintop, and on the journey of the great unknown in between.

Maybe you've never faced a health crisis before. Maybe you've been given the news that you or someone you love has cancer. Or maybe you haven't had anything as serious as a cancer diagnosis, but the mess you find yourself in is still painful. My goal isn't to compare your mess with mine or anyone else's. Whether you get a small or a large stain on your shirt, you're still going to change your shirt. The size of the mess isn't what matters; it's about how we address it.

You aren't in your mess on your own. Even when you don't know where you're going, you know who goes with you. We have the promise of peace, from the God of peace, because of the blood that was shed on the cross by the Prince of Peace.

CHAPTER 4

The Gift of Pain and How to Press through It

When John and Tara Blocker welcomed their daughter Ashlyn into the world, they thought she may be the most well-behaved baby of all time. She hardly made a peep. Tara recalled a bad diaper rash Ashlyn had that landed them at the pediatrician's office, but still no tears from Ashlyn. As she got older, anytime she would fall or injure herself, Tara said Ashlyn seemed "happy as can be."[1] She never indicated she was in any kind of pain, even when most people would be.

Ashlyn was diagnosed with congenital insensitivity to pain with anhidrosis (CIPA). CIPA is a rare genetic disorder caused by a gene mutation that hinders the development and transmission signals of sensory neurons to the point where you cannot feel pain.

The Gift of Pain

Good Morning America heard the Blockers' story and flew them to New York. They were then put in touch with Dr. Roland Staud, a professor of medicine and rheumatologist. He found mutations in Ashlyn's SCN9A gene, which is connected to both severe pain and pain insensitivity. Geoffrey Woods, a medical geneticist at Cambridge University, ended up discovering the connection between the SCN9A gene and an inability to feel pain. In an interview with *The New York Times*, Woods said that he heard of a boy that couldn't feel pain. He went to see him, but before he could, the boy died. "For his birthday, he'd wanted to do something for his friends—he'd wanted to jump off the first-floor roof of his house. And he did. And he got up and said he was fine and died a day later because of a hemorrhage. I realized that pain had a different meaning than I had thought."[2]

Pain is unpleasant, yes, but it is an unexpected gift. Without it, we're unable to detect danger, even if it's present. It may not always feel like it, but medically speaking, pain is a gift, and I would submit to you that spiritually speaking, pain is a gift as well.

The messiness in our lives is either the offspring of pain or the catalyst for pain. But even when we come to understand that messes and suffering are certainties in a sinful world, it doesn't make them any less painful. If I know somebody is going to punch me in the face, it's still going to hurt. Just because I know it's coming doesn't mean it won't be painful; it simply means I'll be prepared. If we look carefully, though, we'll find that quite often our wounds become great sources of wisdom.

In 1 Corinthians 1:22–25, Paul says, "The Jews ask for signs and the Greeks seek wisdom, but we preach Christ crucified, a stumbling block to the Jews and foolishness to the Gentiles. Yet to those who are called, both Jews and Greeks, Christ is the power of God and the wisdom of God, because God's foolishness is wiser than human wisdom, and God's weakness is stronger than human strength" (CSB).

The Jews wanted signs that the Messiah had come to deliver them. Greeks sought wisdom, celebrating academics, philosophy, reasoning, and oration. In a crucified Christ, the Jews saw the opposite of powerful deliverance and the Greeks saw the opposite of reason and wisdom.

For those who don't know Jesus, they see Him on the cross and see God as foolish for getting into that mess and weak for allowing it to happen. But for those who know Jesus, we see that He went to the cross with a wisdom we couldn't understand and that He overcame sin and death by a power we couldn't comprehend. The mess of the cross is a powerful sign of deliverance and wisdom beyond reason. It is by His wounds that we receive power and wisdom and are healed. Jesus's pain and suffering were a gift to us. Maybe our pain is a gift as well, and because of Him, we can press through it.

Pain and Comfort

The ancient city of Corinth was a major city in southern Greece. As an epicenter for trade, it was a diverse city and a wealthy commercial and social power. As a result, it was influenced by many cultures. Paul had to preach Jesus over other gods, idols, and worldviews, often at the expense of his own suffering.

Paul knows the Corinthians share in his sufferings and writes to encourage them:

> Blessed be the God and Father of our Lord Jesus Christ, the Father of mercies and God of all comfort, who comforts us in all our affliction, so that we may be able to comfort those who are in any affliction, with the comfort with which we ourselves are comforted by God. For as we share abundantly in Christ's sufferings, so through Christ we share abundantly in comfort too. If we are afflicted, it is for your comfort and salvation; and if we are comforted, it is for your comfort, which you experience when you patiently endure the same sufferings that we suffer. Our hope for you in unshaken, for we know that as you share in our sufferings, you will also share in our comfort.
>
> 2 Corinthians 1:3–7 ESV

In those five verses we read the word "comfort" ten times. For those of you who aren't mathematicians, that's two mentions per verse. You can't know comfort if you've never known affliction. Comfort is only understood in light of pain and distress. For us to get to a place of comfort, we have to move from a place of discomfort. This is true of all of life's messes, from the most trivial of discomforts to the most devastating pains. I appreciate the comfort of socks that don't slide down because I've known the annoyance of socks that do slide down with each step. And I can appreciate the comfort of health because I've known the pain of my health hanging in the balance.

The last two verses of this passage in 1 Corinthians say, "If we are afflicted, it is for your comfort and salvation; and if we are comforted, it is for your comfort, which you experience when you patiently endure the same sufferings that we suffer. Our hope for you is unshaken, for we know that *as you share in our sufferings, you will also share in our comfort*" (emphasis added). Comfort and suffering are inextricably linked, and that isn't a coincidence. Comfort cannot be present where pain has been absent. Where there is suffering, there can be soothing. Where there is soothing, there is a Savior. He is not only a God who brings comfort; He is the God of all comfort.

Wedding Day Disaster

A few days before my wedding, I was traveling. Admittedly, it was a bold decision. Lindsey had let me know in no uncertain terms that if I missed the rehearsal dinner there would be no consummating the marriage. Luckily, I arrived home on time. I went to bed the night before our wedding feeling relaxed, but when I woke up the next morning, well . . . that's a different story.

When my eyes opened, my head felt as though it had a heartbeat—I could feel it pulsing. I could smell food being made in the kitchen, and just the smell of it made me throw up. Today of all days? Was it nerves? I didn't know. My family tried to keep it close to the vest, but I couldn't seem to shake it. I kept thinking, "What is happening to me right now?" When it came time for the first look, I walked with our photographer, but she had to hold my hand to lead me and rubbed my back as I started dry heaving behind a tree. I had to close my eyes the entire way because of the sun; the light made me nauseous.

I suffer from migraines every so often; I typically get a

couple of them each year. The timing couldn't have been worse. One of our friends who is a doctor went from table to table asking for medication to try and get me back to normal, because at our reception, I couldn't even eat. It wasn't until we got to our hotel room that night that I felt better. Funny how that works.

I'll never forget lying in my room before the ceremony started. I lay in darkness with a cold rag over my eyes, and I prayed out loud, "Today of all days, Lord? Really?" But it was one of those rare moments when I felt as though God was literally beside me. I couldn't hear an audible voice, but I felt as if He was whispering to my heart, reminding me that it was a big day, but that He couldn't get my attention any other way. I had been so busy doing things for God that I hadn't actually spent much time with Him. For half an hour, I just prayed. I poured out my heart for Lindsey, our marriage, my insecurities, dreams, and goals, as we began to live life on mission together for Him. It was incredible. This sounds insane, but I could feel the comfort of God. I didn't walk down that aisle alone; He walked with me.

When people hear this story they'll say, "That's awful that the biggest day of your life was ruined," but my perspective on the pain of that day has shifted. I puked all day, felt like my head would explode, and had the mobility of a cinderblock. But on the biggest day of my life, as I entered a new covenantal relationship, I was reminded that the covenant-keeping God was entering it with me. I wouldn't change the circumstances of that day for anything. Sometimes our stories of suffering and God's comfort in them aren't always for our own faith, but for strengthening the faith of others. As Paul reminds us in 2 Corinthians 1:4–5 (ESV), "[God], who comforts us in all our affliction, so that we may be able to comfort those who are in any affliction, with the comfort with which we ourselves are comforted by God. For as we share abundantly in Christ's sufferings, so through Christ we share abundantly in comfort too."

Life has highs and lows, and suffering is a part of that cyclical process. If everything went the way we wanted it to, we would have no need for faith. Through the highs and lows, suffering and comfort, we are in a constant state of dependence on God and we're given the opportunity to tell others about the experiences we've had in walking with the Lord. What God pours into our lives is meant to be poured out to others.

Nobody connects to a story without struggle. You don't go see a movie about a guy who drives to work in his Range Rover, builds his 401(k), eats a meal with his perfect family in his perfect house, and then repeats it all the next day. You love a story where you can connect with the struggle. In *The Notebook*, if Allie doesn't struggle through Alzheimer's and Noah doesn't comfort her through it by faithfully reading their story to her, it wouldn't be as powerful! In *Gladiator*, if Maximus doesn't suffer through the pains of injustice and the murder of his family before becoming the gladiator who comforts the oppressed by killing corruption, it wouldn't be as powerful! Stories of struggle are powerful and widely shared with the world because we love to see that even in our struggles, there is hope. And that hope is contagious.

But if we're honest with ourselves, in the middle of the painful messiness of life, we don't necessarily care how, why, or what God is utilizing our struggles for. We just want them to end. We would do anything to alleviate our pain rather than being comforted in our pain.

God's Operating Table

In college I got to watch a surgeon at work, and I've never been more intrigued by a process in my life. The tray laid out, the instruments sterilized, the preparation and precision—the process was immaculate. Suppose you had to explain surgery to someone who didn't understand it. Cutting someone open while they're "sleeping" on a freezing cold table? That sounds like the most psychotic thing ever! On the surface, you would think doctors are sick-minded people who carve people like pumpkins. But when you explain that the person is sick, and the only way to fix the brokenness inside them is to cut them open, what once seemed psychotic is clearly a strategic mission to save.

Is surgery invasive? Yes. Will you be sore afterward? Yes. But does it ultimately lead to life? You better believe it. A scalpel in the hands of someone who intends to do harm is life threatening, but a scalpel in the hands of a skilled surgeon is life giving. In the hands of a good surgeon, I know that regardless of any pain I may feel, the surgeon's hands are steady, and their goal is to bring me life. I may not understand every cut, but I know it's for my good. Sometimes God will allow pain in your life to bring healing in areas you didn't even know were broken. Those cuts bring us pain, but the goal of that pain is ultimately to bring healing.

Asking God to eradicate our pain is the natural cry of our hearts. We hate the brokenness of a world tainted by sin, and we long for heaven. In Jesus, our story doesn't begin at birth and end in death; it begins at crucifixion and ends in resurrection. During the time Jesus walked this earth, the cross wasn't seen the way believers see it now. It was a humiliating instrument of death, but because of Jesus, our perspective has changed.

Where some see a gruesome instrument of death used to torture and humiliate, we see the way to life, through the mess of the cross, the key that allows comfort to come through the door of suffering. We can look at the suffering of the cross and see the glory of the resurrection.

I read this poem by Robert Browning Hamilton the other day, and it struck a chord with me:

> I walked a mile with Pleasure;
> She chattered all the way;
> But left me none the wiser
> For all she had to say.
>
> I walked a mile with Sorrow,
> and ne'er a word said she;
> But, oh! The things I learned from her,
> when Sorrow walked with me.[3]

Often God's greatest lessons are presented to us in our pain. Paul knew pain, yet he praised God as his comforter in 2 Corinthians 1:3 (ESV): "Blessed be the God and Father of our Lord Jesus Christ, the Father of mercies and God of all comfort." He is the God of all comfort, and His comforting presence is more palpable in our pain. He comforts us in our messes, but He also helps us to press through them.

By Grace and . . . CrossFit

I've always been active, but one summer I came home from college and noticed that I wasn't in the greatest shape. I had developed an unwanted inner tube around my midsection. I don't know why, but that semester had gotten the best of me. It was to the point where I'd walk up a normal flight of stairs but feel as if I were competing in an IRONMAN triathlon. I had to do my best to make sure nobody could hear how hard I was breathing.

My insecurities were magnified when Alex walked into the kitchen without a shirt on. Even though we're siblings, Alex and I look nothing alike. He has blond hair and blue eyes. I have brown hair and brown eyes. He was always stout and chubby. I was always tall and skinny. So I was shocked when Alex walked in at about six feet four, long blond hair sashaying around his shoulders, and a body that looked like it had been chiseled by angels.

"What's up, bro? How was the semester?"

He didn't address the fact that he looked like Thor, so finally I answered, "Fine, yours?"

"Good. Glad it's over, though. I'm going to work out. You're welcome to join."

"Is that how that happened?"

"How what happened?"

"*That!*" I pointed to his torso area, "*All* of *that*! I don't even know what some of those muscles are!" Feeling somewhat apprehensive but also aware of the lack of bumps protruding from my body, I accepted his invitation. I didn't realize that I had just signed up for my first experience with CrossFit.

As we walked into the gym, I felt like the new kid in school. The class before us was wrapping up, and I wondered if we had missed the door to the gym and stopped by a local torture chamber. People were doing things that I didn't even know were humanly possible. I wasn't sure if people were working out or performing exorcisms. A lady started screaming while lifting, and I ran over to her. "Ma'am, are you okay?"

Alex pulled me aside and covered for me, "Dude! She's just lifting."

"It sounded like she was screaming in pain to me, but agree to disagree."

I kept seeing the acronym W.A.Y.M.O., so I asked Alex, "What does W.A.Y.M.O. stand for?"

"It's what they call this CrossFit class. It stands for What Are You Made Of."

I thought, "Are you sure it's not Whatever These Psychopaths Are Made Of?"

That wasn't the only new lingo I picked up on that day; it's like these people were speaking a different language. They were asking me questions I didn't understand, like, "Hey, man. What's your push press max?"

"My what? Who is Max?"

I'll tell you this because at this point I've dealt with it, emo tionally. During that workout, my life flashed before my eyes. I was within a heartbeat or two of cardiac arrest. That next morning when I woke up, I tried to get out of bed, but I don't think I saw another human being for a few days. I could hardly move my limbs. The next week, Alex asked me if I wanted to go again. I contemplated his offer for a moment, but I agreed, and by the end of summer, I went every day and built muscles in places that I didn't even know you could grow muscles. Why? Because I kept going. Not when I felt good enough to go, not when the pain subsided, but through the pain my body experienced. I was a mess for a few weeks, but once I recognized that I could push through the pain, I saw extraordinary growth.

Your ability to persevere through hardship will determine the power of your impact. Not the size of your platform, not the people around you, and not the potential within you, but your ability to persevere and endure suffering. You can press through the pain, not just for the sake of the gospel, but by the very power of the gospel. We can each probably identify a mess in our life that was particularly painful, one we've suffered through and wondered whether there is any way we'll be able to get through it. Thankfully, because of Jesus and by the Holy Spirit, we have the power to endure pain and persevere through it.

In 2 Timothy, Paul gets deeply personal. He is imprisoned in Rome for the second time, during the reign of Nero, who was persecuting Christians, and Paul knows this is it. He makes it abundantly clear that he has run his race and is about to cross the finish line. He writes to his mentee Timothy, encouraging him to have an unrelenting endurance and perseverance for the gospel, no matter what.

Second Timothy 2:1 (ESV) says, "You then, my child, be strengthened by the grace that is in Christ Jesus." In my experience, most people don't see grace as something that strengthens us, but it does. Grace isn't just a one-time gift; it continually gives us the strength to press through the pain of our suffering. We're not strengthened by just any grace—not the grace given to you by people around you or people who follow you—and it isn't something that you can dig deep and find within yourself. It's the very grace of God, given to us through Jesus, that strengthens us. How much more boldly would we live our lives if we weren't simply aware of the gift of grace but lived a life strengthened by it?

Paul knows a thing or two about living a life strengthened by grace. In Acts 14 he is stoned at Lystra and left for dead. Later, by the strength of the grace available to him in Christ, he goes back and preaches to the same city that stoned him. He encourages other believers, saying, "We must go through many hardships to enter the kingdom of God" (v. 22).

In 2 Corinthians 12, Paul says that he was given a thorn in his flesh, a messenger of Satan, to torment him. But when he pleaded with Jesus to take it away, Jesus said, "My grace is sufficient for you, for my power is made perfect in weakness" (v. 9). Sometimes the enemy keeps you safe by pushing you further into the arms of Christ unintentionally. He tries to keep you from your calling and creates a mess in your life because he knows it will frustrate you. But in His sovereignty, God allows that to happen because He knows that seasons of frustration are a fertile time of preparation. God will allow Satan to send storms, but what Satan intends to use to sink you, God strategically utilizes to water the seeds of your sanctification. You will have moments when you feel overwhelmed, but you will not be overcome, because of the grace that strengthens you in Jesus.

Transformation Is in the Trial

In 2 Timothy 2:3–6 (ESV), Paul says, "Share in suffering as a good soldier of Christ Jesus. No soldier gets entangled in civilian pursuits, since his aim is to please the one who enlisted him. An athlete is not crowned unless he competes according to the rules. It is the hard-working farmer who ought to have the first share of the crops." He gives examples of professions that don't seem to have much in common, but when you look deeper, they all require perseverance. To celebrate victory, the soldier has to keep fighting. To celebrate victory, the athlete has to keep running. To celebrate victory, the farmer has to keep working. Charles Spurgeon once said,

> There is no glory in being a featherbed soldier, a man bedecked with gorgeous medals, but never beautified by a scar, or ennobled by a wound. All that you ever hear of such a soldier is that his spurs jingle on the pavement as he walks. There is no history for this carpet knight. He is just a dandy. He never smelled gunpowder in battle in his life. If he did, he fetched out his cologne to kill the offensive odor. Oh, if we could be wise enough to choose, even were as wise as the Lord Himself, we would choose the troubles which He has appointed to us, and we would not spare ourselves a single pang.[4]

We need endurance and perseverance, the determination to press through the mess. It may be painful, but our goal is to be good soldiers of Christ, to follow Him into any and every circumstance for God's glory. We must be bold and unrelenting in our efforts to push the kingdom of God forward against the darkness. Delicacy doesn't win wars, but perseverance always prevails. If you're breathing and reading this right now, you're still in the fight, and if you're still in the fight, you can struggle well. If you've enlisted in the army of Christ, victory is yours, but that doesn't mean you're exempt from fighting in the trenches. Be an outstanding soldier of Christ. Hold on to your cross, even when it hurts. Because your trials are transforming you.

Becoming the Katana

In ancient Japan the samurai were warriors without equal, and their weapon was the katana. The katana is not your average sword. Ian Bottomley, curator emeritus of Oriental Collections at Britain's Royal Armouries, said, "It has everything the perfect weapon should have."[5] The samurai even believed it had a soul of its own, and that the only way a samurai's soul could be separated from the soul of their sword was by death. Like I said, not your average sword. The process of making a katana was way ahead of its time. For three days and nights, ten men wouldn't sleep as they carefully combined iron, carbon, and charcoal in a massive furnace heated to over one thousand degrees Celsius. This allowed impurities in the elements to fall to the floor of the furnace, leaving a pure steel called *tamahagane*. The finest pieces of *tamahagane* were then sent to a swordsmith, and for more than three months, they would craft it into a blade. It would be reheated, turned over, and hammered into shape. Finally, it was sent to someone who professionally sharpened and polished the blade, giving it a unique look and finish, which could also take months.

Japanese sword makers managed to create a nearly perfect steel. Just enough carbon was retained to make the inside of the blade soft, giving it the ability to withstand attackers, and just enough iron was retained on the outside of the blade to make it razor sharp, making it effective for attacking. It took dozens of men and more than six months to create the perfect mixture of toughness and softness, a hard-cutting edge and a soft flexible core. You couldn't simply order a katana for recreational use. It's not like if you had the money and were in the market for a large butter knife you could order one. The katana wasn't a trophy you could win; it was a prize you must earn. That's what made the katana so intimidating—not only that it was the perfect weapon but also because of whose hands the weapon was in. The enemy knew that if their opponent had a katana, they had signed up for a life of perseverance, discipline, and training. It made the samurai elite.

This is where the sword makers got it right and culture gets it wrong. Culture tells us that carbon and steel can't intermingle, that we can't become *tamahagane.* When facing painful messes, people are taught to become one of two things:

1. They become so hard that they hurt themselves or others, and really, their sharpness is a way of hiding how brittle they are. If they get attacked, they break easily.
2. They become so soft that they learn to be offended by everything, and as bad as they want to make an impact, they aren't strong enough to leave a lasting mark.

We don't have to choose between being hard or soft; *tamahagane* is the best of both. We can maintain our hard edge and remain strong in our convictions and faith. That edge allows us to make an impact for what and whom we believe in, without becoming brittle, because we can simultaneously tap into our soft core. In the midst of our messiness, our sharp edge isn't what defines us. It's a tool to carry our heart's mission, which is to love people. A soft core leads us to love, and that love leads us to use our hard-cutting edge to advance the truth of who God is and what He is doing.

My prayer is that we would have a hard-cutting edge, sharp

enough to make an impact in the fight against our messes and war against our pains, but also that we would have a soft core, so that we can absorb hits from the enemy—the messiness and pains of life. A good soldier needs a good weapon, and the truly perfect weapon is the grace that strengthens us in Christ. It gives us thick skin, a soft heart, and a sharp mind. We need a tough exterior that never fears the truth, a soft core governed by our love for God and people, and a sharp mind to discern the proper strategies for different battles.

Just as the katana isn't formed overnight, we too are formed into something beautiful when we learn to trust God in our trials. It takes perseverance. Paul's preaching at Lystra was probably more impactful when he had persevered through the stoning that left him for dead. His commitment to Christ was probably strengthened by the grace that helped him persevere through the thorn in his flesh. The power of your impact for the kingdom will be more profound as you persevere in the messiness of life, by the power and grace of the gospel.

Press through the Pain

We all want breakthrough. We want to break through the pain and the mess, but we don't really talk about how breakthrough occurs. It's easy to say, "God will bring breakthrough!" Yes, that's true. But we have to accept that breakthrough doesn't avoid pain; it attacks it. Jesus says, "My power is made perfect in weakness" (2 Corinthians 12:9). Not over, around, or under your weakness, but in it. His power meets us in our messes, our darkest moments, worst fears, and painful places. Breakthrough occurs when His grace strengthens us in our pain, pushes us through the pain, and breaks through beyond our pain. Rumi, the Persian poet, said, "The wound is the place where the Light enters you."[6] Often in our darkest trials, we find the light of Christ. You can't press through what you won't press into. Your pain isn't the absence of God's presence; it's where you discover that His power is made perfect in your weakness.

In 2 Corinthians 1:8–10, Paul describes a struggle they faced. "We do not want you to be uninformed, brothers and sisters, about the troubles we experienced in the province of Asia. We were under great pressure, far beyond our ability to endure, so that we despaired of life itself. Indeed, we felt we had received the sentence of death. But this happened that we might not rely on ourselves but on God, who raises the dead. He has delivered us from such a deadly peril, and he will deliver us again. On him we have set our hope that he will continue to deliver us."

They couldn't rely on their own strength. The grace of God was their strength to get them through their mess, and it's enough to get you through your mess. Paul says that they were delivered. God will deliver you too. Even when you fear that this is the mess you won't be able to conquer, God is continually delivering you. He has done it before, and He will continue to do it.

CHAPTER 5

You Can't Win the War on Your Own

The exodus is one of the most epic and captivating stories not only in Scripture but in all human history. Everyone knows the story of Moses and God's miraculous deliverance of Israel. God brings the ten plagues against Egypt, and after the final plague in which all Egypt's firstborn are killed, Pharaoh lets Moses and the Israelites go free after four hundred years of enslavement. As the Israelites are making this mass exodus, Pharaoh's heart is hardened. He changes his mind and pursues the Israelites with his army, but God is with Israel, and He splits the Red Sea so that they can cross safely on dry ground, while the Egyptians are subsequently drowned. That's about where we end the story. God works a miracle, Pharaoh's army is destroyed, and the Israelites go camping in the wilderness for forty years, singing "Kumbaya." But the story doesn't end there. You don't have to go much further in Exodus before stumbling upon a lesser known but equally powerful chapter in the story of God's deliverance. Just three chapters after God splits the sea, in Exodus 17:8–13, the Israelites find themselves in another messy situation.

> The Amalekites came and attacked the Israelites at Rephidim. Moses said to Joshua, "Choose some of our men and go out to fight the Amalekites. Tomorrow I will stand on top of the hill with the staff of God in my hands."
>
> So Joshua fought the Amalekites as Moses had ordered, and Moses, Aaron and Hur went to the top of the hill. As long as Moses held up his hands, the Israelites were winning, but whenever he lowered his hands, the Amalekites were winning. When Moses' hands grew tired, they took a stone and put it under him and he sat on it. Aaron and Hur held his hands up—one on one side, one on the other—so that his hands remained steady till sunset. So Joshua overcame the Amalekite army with the sword.

Do you notice who instigates? The Amalekites attack the Israelites. Even though God is with Israel, the Amalekites come in uninvited and ambush the Israelites. If you're anything like me, you have moments when someone or something comes in uninvited and creates a mess in your life that throws you off the path you were trying to follow. You think, "God, I thought You were with me. What are You doing? Why am I in this mess? I didn't even bring it on myself this time!"

But that's where we have it all wrong. Walking with God doesn't entitle us to a barrier between us and our battles. In fact, it often puts a bull's-eye on our back, and the enemy takes aim.

Are you praying that God will keep trials from you, or are you praying that God will equip you for the trials you have to face? Our impact is only as great as our involvement in the battle, and as the people of God, we want to be destined for great impact, so we must be equipped.

The story in Exodus 17:8–13 is the first battle the Israelites face after God miraculously delivers them from Egypt. It's completely out of the blue and completely unprovoked. They have hardly begun their journey from Egypt to the Promised Land, and as they are trying to pass from the chains of slavery in Egypt to the freedom of new life in the Promised Land, they are ambushed. There are more aspects to the battles we face than we realize. Joshua carries out the physical, tangible battle plan that is needed to conquer the enemy, but an even more important strategy needs to be carried out—a spiritual strategy.

The Lion King and the King of Kings

When I was growing up, I'm fairly certain that my level of television and movie consumption was borderline unhealthy. I remember watching things that I didn't even enjoy much. But I've always loved the idea of story, watching it creatively play out even if it wasn't great. I did have a few that I latched on to, though, none more than Disney's *The Lion King*. We all know how it opens. That song is unmistakably *Lion King*. I didn't, and still don't, understand a single word being sung, but I would sing along as if I knew every word, slowly rising off my couch like I too was making my way to Pride Rock.

I loved this movie, and I still do. I watched it recently and had different takeaways than I did as a child. As a kid, I only saw parts of a movie coming together, but now I see the purpose behind the plot. This is a redemption story, a story of surrender, a story of liberation, and a tale of the importance of help in unlikely places from unlikely friends.

In the beginning that crazy baboon, Rafiki, holds up the young lion cub, Simba, and all the animals bow. Why? Because a promise is being made. This young lion is being dedicated to the promises that have been spoken over his life by his father, Mufasa, including that one day he will rule as the king.

But it isn't long before tragedy strikes. In one of the saddest moments, not only in Disney history but in cinematic history, Mufasa dies in a stampede, trying to save his child. Simba is telling his dad to get up, but it isn't happening. He starts crying, I start crying, we all start crying, and Simba runs away. Why? Because of the guilt and shame he feels after being convinced it's his fault that his father is dead. The plot thickens!

After Timon and Pumba rescue Simba, it looks as though he is living the good life in paradise with his friends. *Hakuna matata*, right? But deep down something is missing, and he knows it. Simba's friend Nala finally challenges him to deal with the problems of his past. Why? To face the fear, guilt, shame, and insecurities of feeling like it's his fault that his father is dead, that he's a failure for running away, and that he's unworthy to walk in his calling. Things were clearly simpler before he met his love interest. Some of us can relate.

Eventually Simba runs into Rafiki again, and the whole movie turns. Rafiki helps Simba see his father within himself and reminds Simba of who he is, not what he has done. He reminds him of the promises his father had spoken over him as a child, and in that moment, Simba surrenders all the guilt, shame, fear, insecurity, unworthiness, and feelings of failure.

Uninvited enemies in Simba's life had kept him from walking in the promises of his father, but his eventual willingness to surrender brought liberation from those enemies and gave him the freedom to walk in his father's promises. Simba's story isn't unlike your story or my story, and it isn't unlike the story we read in Exodus 17. If we surrender, we can walk in the promises and the victory that God has given us in Jesus.

Break Free and Bring Friends

Many of you are trying to break free from the messes you find yourselves in and begin a new life in the Promised Land. You've camped in the promises of God, but uninvited enemies ambush you and keep you from holding on to those promises.

Those uninvited enemies look different for everyone. Many of you get ambushed by the enemy of insecurity. You're insecure that you aren't an adequate parent or spouse. You're insecure that you'll never find someone who loves you or about what other people think of you. It consumes you. You feel ambushed by the enemies of guilt and shame. Your past isn't going away as easily as you thought it would, and it's eating at your sanity. Anxiety is ambushing you. Fear is running in and attacking your camp.

Maybe you wanted to step out in faith and do that thing you've always dreamed of doing, but fear dressed itself up as the responsible thing to do. Now you're living the life that pleases people around you, and you've made it look like you're loving it, but on the inside you're miserable.

Maybe you've been hiding a secret sin in your life, and you've put so much time into trying to hide it that it has kept you from people you love and people who love you, and it has been ambushing you when you least expect it. You wonder what people would think if they knew. It's assaulting your thoughts and taking you away from the important things in your life.

Maybe you read that and think, "Yes! That's me. But how do I continue to move forward in the promises of God, in the victory that I have been given through Jesus, when I am constantly fighting off uninvited enemies in my life?" I'd tell you to look at Moses's response to Amalek invading.

Moses sends Joshua to lead the battle on the ground and tells him, "I will stand on the top of the hill with the staff of God in my hands" (Exodus 17:9). Then he goes to the top of the hill, but he doesn't go alone. Moses brings Aaron and Hur, two of the people closest to him. He knows it's going to be a difficult fight. He anticipates that he is going to have moments when he is struggling, so he comes prepared for the battle that he has yet to face. He brings his friends.

When Moses holds his hands up, the Israelites prevail, but when his hands fall, the Amalekites prevail. When Moses grows sluggish, Aaron and Hur bring him a stone to sit on and steady his hands until Israel overwhelms the enemy. Our hands are going to grow weary, and we will slip. We want to have patient, unshakable faith at all times, but there is much to endure along the way. We need friends who will bring us a stone to sit on and hold our arms up so that we can continue the fight and prevail toward the promise.

Sometimes we hear a verse so often that I think the power of it gets lost in its popularity. Proverbs 27:17 (CSB) says, "Iron sharpens iron, and one person sharpens another." When we bring our friends to stand with us in the fight for faith, a few things happen. Much like when we rub two blades together. It helps keep the shine of the blade, and it also helps the blade maintain its sharpness. This is why Moses brings Aaron and Hur with him to the top of the hill, and this is why it is imperative that you bring friends with you in your walk with the Lord. They help you shine brighter for the Lord because they refuse to let your blade become dull, and they help sharpen your blade for the battles in your life as they fight alongside you. Moses gets weary, just as he had anticipated, but he was prepared. His arms began to fall, his blade was losing its shine and its sharpness, but his friends were there to help him continue toward the promise.

God brought them into a new land, the Promised Land, but it wouldn't be without its fair share of challenges. God doesn't promise us that we are exempt from the messiness of life but that He will be with us in the messiness of life. And He often places people around us to help us along the way. We need people in our lives who will pick us up when we don't have the strength to stand. Moses is aware of something we all need to be aware of—if you want to win small battles, fight alone. You'll move faster. If you want to win wars, fight together. You'll go further. Bring your friends.

Leaping into Liberation

One summer, when I was a kid, my family and our extended relatives got together and decided to spend some time on the lake. We rented a massive pontoon boat and enjoyed the warm summer day. It was perfect. There was just enough wind to relieve you from the heat, but just enough sun to get a tan without feeling as though your skin was melting off. We came to a cove encircled by enormous cliffs. I was taking it all in when my attention was redirected. I watched as a teenage boy got a running start before jumping off the largest cliff in the cove. He took flight. I stood up in my seat as I watched him lose momentum. His body lost the fight with gravity, and he came crashing toward the water but somehow managed to execute a flawless cannonball.

All the guys in our family raced out of the boat and began ascending the cliff, preparing to jump off it. One by one my cousins, uncles, dad, and brother all began to take flight. As I watched my cousins leap off this cliff, I remember being struck by their apparent fearlessness of plummeting to their death. As an eleven-year-old, I was terrified at the prospect of flinging myself from this cliff I had never been on, into a lake I had never been in. Finally my dad jumped, then my brother, and I was the last one up.

People started coming up to jump a second time, and I still hadn't even made an attempt. I felt dumb. Everyone else leaped with no issue. I remember looking just over the cliff face, trying to weigh the monumental risks and minimal rewards. My dad looked up at me from the water, calling for me to jump. I couldn't do it. I was embarrassed. At this point, everyone who had jumped was lining up single file behind me. I turned and made my way to the back of the line, shoulders slumped, head low. I looked up and saw that my dad was waiting there. If I wasn't embarrassed enough before, now it took everything in me not to cry. I was insecure that I was the only one who hadn't jumped and wondered what others were thinking of me. I was paralyzed by fear, but my dad bent down and hugged me.

"Luke, you can do this, you just have to let go and go for it. I know it's a little scary, but it's not as bad as it looks. What if I jump with you?" He took me to the cliff, and we looked over it together. He pointed to an area where he thought we should make our landing, counted to three, and hand in hand, we leaped.

Although I'm young in that memory, it's still powerful to me. The enemies I faced on that cliff are still real today; they've just manifested themselves in different ways. I don't fear jumping off a cliff, but I fear jumping into the unknown. I don't feel insecure if others jump into a lake that I don't want to jump into, but I do feel insecure if others jump into new territory that I've lacked the faith to jump into. I don't feel embarrassed if I have to head to the back of a line where others are running off a cliff, but I do feel embarrassed if I'm at the back of a line where others are doing things that I feel like I can't do.

The most powerful thing about that memory is that I can still feel the liberation of the jump. I surrendered all the fears I faced into the arms of my father. He sought me out and promised me that it was going to be more than fine because he was going to jump with me. Surrendering my fears allowed me to run into my father's promises and leap confidently into a new experience with him.

Victory in Surrender

Moses sends Joshua to fight the battle on the ground, but the victory comes through prayer and surrender. Moses lifts his hands up in prayer and surrender to the Lord. You have to hold up in surrender what is holding you back, or you'll have a difficult time walking in the promise of victory that you've been given in Christ. Surrendering your burdens to Jesus allows you to move forward, because it lightens the burden you carry and allows you to run freely.

I love The Message version of 2 Corinthians 10:4: "We use our powerful God-tools for smashing warped philosophies, tearing down barriers erected against the truth of God, fitting every loose thought and emotion and impulse into the structure of life shaped by Christ. Our tools are ready at hand for clearing the ground of every obstruction and building lives of obedience into maturity."

What is holding you back that you need to surrender? What barriers need to be torn down in your life that go against the truth of God? The truth of God is that you have been promised salvation by grace through faith in Jesus, a new life in Christ, and that the sins you can't forget, God refuses to remember because of what Jesus did for you and me on the cross. Some of you read that and are probably thinking, "Well, that all sounds great, Luke, but it's harder than you make it seem. I know Jesus, but I'm still dealing with my mess. I'm still dealing with insecurity, fear, anxiety, and shame. I'm still struggling with lust; I'm still battling these addictions; I'm still broken-hearted. Maybe this is something that I'll just have to learn to deal with. Other people will get to live freely, but I'm used to lugging these chains around. I've done it for so long."

Here is the truth: we all want the victory, but we don't always want to fight the battle. You can't win a battle you refuse to fight. If you want the victory, you have to fight the opposition, and the greatest weapons you have are prayer and surrender. In *My Utmost for His Highest*, Oswald Chambers says, "If you are faced with the question of whether or not to surrender, make a determination to go on through the crisis, surrendering all that you have and all that you are to Him. And God will then equip you to do all that He requires of you."[1] Surrender all of yourself to God so that He can equip you to do all that He has called you to.

I've got good news and I've got bad news. Let's start with the bad news first. The bad news is that you can't win the war. You can't, not on your own. The good news is that Jesus has already won the war. The victory has already been secured, but you would be wise to bring friends that will help you along the way.

Can I let you in on something? God is not a God of partial victory. Your mess doesn't get any piece of you, because all of you has been purchased by the blood of Christ. He gets the victory over everything. First Corinthians 15:57 (ESV) says, "Thanks be to God, who gives us the victory through our Lord Jesus Christ." It doesn't say, "Thanks be to God, who gives us some victory, or partial victory, or victory every now and then." It says, "Thanks be to God, who gives us *the* victory through our Lord Jesus Christ" (emphasis added). There is no mess in your life, no sin that you grapple with, that Jesus isn't Lord of and Lord over. He is greater and more powerful than any mess, sin, and circumstance that you could surrender to Him. Jesus didn't come to offer discounts; He came and paid off all debts.

It's interesting if you think about it. The Israelites secured their first victory on their way to the Promised Land as Moses stretched his arms out with the staff of God in his hands. Similarly, yet greater, is that the victory of the promise of salvation was secured when Jesus stretched His arms out on the cross, as He stood in our place and bore our sins on that tree.

Imagine this. As Joshua and the Israelite army are on the ground, recognizing that they've just defeated the Amalekites, the Bible tells us that the sun is going down. They shift their gaze from their defeated foes to the top of the hill and see Moses with Aaron and Hur on either side of him, holding his arms up. It is then they realize that Moses's surrender secured the victory. Many years later people would look on a hill where the Son of God, Jesus Christ, was crucified with two men on either side of him, and now we can look back in time and see that it was there, on that hill, at that moment in history, that God poured Himself out to secure the victory that saved us.

Jesus gives us the victory. You are no longer a slave to your circumstances and situations. Death could not hold Him. Sin could not shake Him; it was killed and buried with Him in the tomb. When Jesus walked out of that tomb, He walked out with the keys to the grave, and He has set you free from all the messes you feel are holding you back from experiencing Him. You aren't fighting for victory; you are already walking in victory. You aren't fighting for acceptance; you can worship because you have been accepted. You don't have to earn a room in the house or a seat at the table; you've already got one through the finished work of Jesus.

Rip the Roof Off

One of my favorite stories in all of Scripture is found in multiple gospel accounts, but I want to look at it specifically through the lens of Mark's gospel. In Mark 2 Jesus has just returned from preaching and teaching in Galilee to His ministry basecamp in Capernaum, and while He is teaching, something unexpected happens. "A few days later, when Jesus again entered Capernaum, the people heard that he had come home. They gathered in such large numbers that there was no room left, not even outside the door, and he preached the word to them" (Mark 2:1–2). It's worth mentioning that in Luke's account of this story, he tells us, "Pharisees and teachers of the law were sitting there. They had come from every village of Galilee and from Judea and Jerusalem" (Luke 5:17). Jesus's fame had spread like wildfire. Everyone has come to listen to Him, even the Pharisees and Sadducees. There is no room in the house, not even outside the door. It is packed.

"Some men came, bringing to him a paralyzed man, carried by four of them. Since they could not get him to Jesus because of the crowd, they made an opening in the roof above Jesus by digging through it and then lowered the mat the man was lying on" (Mark 2:3–4). Here is a messy situation. Not only are these men carrying their paralyzed friend an unknown distance, but homes in ancient Israel were made with flat roofs that were composed of mostly mud and branches. This is a messy job. There are no power tools or precision. People inside the home are being covered with dried mud and other materials. You also have to keep in mind that it's not as if these friends are interrupting a quiet meal; this is a massive gathering. Everyone is there. At best, the friends are embarrassing themselves. At worst, they look like lunatics.

Scripture says in Mark 2:5–13,

> When Jesus saw their faith, he said to the paralyzed man, "Son, your sins are forgiven."
>
> Now some teachers of the law were sitting there, thinking to themselves, "Why does this fellow talk like that? He's blaspheming! Who can forgive sins but God alone?"

> Immediately Jesus knew in his spirit that this was what they were thinking in their hearts, and he said to them, "Why are you thinking these things? Which is easier: to say to this paralyzed man, 'Your sins are forgiven,' or to say, 'Get up, take your mat and walk'? But I want you to know that the Son of Man has authority on earth to forgive sins." So he said to the man, "I tell you, get up, take your mat and go home." He got up, took his mat and walked out in full view of them all. This amazed everyone and they praised God, saying, "We have never seen anything like this!"

There's a lot to dissect in this story. It's a testament to the authority of Jesus. It's easy to say the words "your sins are forgiven," but it's miraculous to see a paralyzed man walk after telling him to "take up your bed and go home." That proves Jesus isn't bluffing; He has the authority to forgive sins. But I want to focus on the friends in the story that carry the paralyzed man. I'm sure that as these friends were carrying their paralytic friend to Jesus, they were talking among themselves. "I hope this is easy. I hope He can do this. I hope He will do this." They may have thought they would just waltz in and get a good seat. They had left early enough, but as they got to the house, a crowd flooded well beyond the door of the house.

Sometimes we have the faith to make our way toward the house, but when our path to Jesus is blocked, we don't know what to do. Often it takes the faith of others to help move us forward through the messes of life. The door isn't an option, so now what? Some of us wait, but most of us would turn around. Not these friends. When you can't go through the door, friends lower you through the roof. When your arms grow weary, they bring you a stone to sit on and hold your hands up. The battle was in getting him to the feet of Jesus. The war was in miraculously healing a paralyzed man.

The victory has been won, but if you don't bring your friends, you'll lose many battles. Victory tastes sweetest when sharing it with others. Those friends made a mess, stopped a sermon, destroyed a home, and lowered their friend to Jesus. But did you notice His response? He isn't mad. He's not like, "Guys, let Me finish. I'm on a roll." What does He do? He sees their faith and says, "Your sins are forgiven. Rise, pick up your bed, and go home." When you take a mess to the feet of Jesus, there are no ceilings on what He will do with it. Bring friends that don't stop at the door; bring friends who rip the roof off.

Because that's how the war is won.

CHAPTER 6

Hanging on by a Thread

Robert Smalls was born as a slave to the McKee family in Beaufort, South Carolina, on April 5, 1839. When he was twelve, the family moved to Charleston, where he fell in love with the sea on the Carolina coast and found work as a laborer on the waterfront, becoming as familiar with the Charleston waters as anyone. In 1856 he married his wife, Hannah Jones, who was a slave as well, and they had three children together. Smalls, like most slaves, feared that his family would be sold and ripped apart. He desperately tried to purchase his family's freedom, but he was denied multiple times.

On April 12, 1861, the Civil War began at Fort Sumter in the Charleston Bay. Robert had landed a job on the *Planter,* an old steamboat turned armed Confederate supply ship. As a member of the enslaved crew, his job wasn't glamorous, but he made it worthwhile. For one year Robert diligently worked in the shadows while devising an escape route to freedom. He knew these waters, but he needed to learn everything he could about the *Planter,* its guards, the checkpoints throughout the harbor, and the signals to pass through undetected. He met with the other enslaved crewmen and told them about his plan. It was dangerous—the consequences would be severe if they got caught—but if they didn't try, they would live in slavery for the rest of their lives. The crew was in.

On May 12, 1862, the white officers went ashore to sleep. This was against Confederate military order, but Robert used the officers' disobedience as an opportunity to set his plan into motion. He alerted the crew. Tonight was the night. Robert put the captain's hat on as he and the crew of slaves commandeered the ship. He successfully navigated them through five checkpoints, making sure each signal was correct. His year of patience was paying off. They made one brief stop at a nearby pier to pick up Robert's family and a handful of other slaves. He couldn't buy freedom, but he wouldn't settle for slavery. The *Planter* passed through Fort Sumter before nearing a Union blockade. One of the Union ships nearly fired on the *Planter,* but a white sheet, the signal of surrender, slowly rose up the flagpole. Robert's crew had sailed out of slavery and found themselves on the shores of freedom. The sun began to rise, turning the moonlit water pink. It wasn't just a new day; it was a new life.

The *Planter* provided Union soldiers with guns, ammunition, and Confederate shipping routes and schedules. For Robert, it was just the beginning. His story reached all the way to the White House. He met with President Abraham Lincoln, was financially compensated by the government for bringing the *Planter* to the Union, and went on a speaking tour, recruiting

African Americans to join the Union Army. Smalls fought in the war as well, becoming the first African American Naval Captain. Ironically, he captained the *USS Planter*, the same ship he had commandeered from the Confederate army. He served in both the House and the Senate, and the cherry on top? He ended up purchasing the home where he was born as a slave. The McKees, his former owners, had lost everything during the war, but Robert took them in and provided for them.

Hollywood couldn't write a better script. It's the ultimate rags-to-riches, against-the-odds story. But before Robert made this great escape, he was hanging on by a thread. He and his wife were enslaved, working ridiculous hours, most of their money went to their owners, he had tried to buy his family's freedom without success, and they were living in the middle of a war. But he saw freedom passing in front of him every day as ships sailed the harbor. He hardly had anything he could hold on to for hope, but with the little faith he had left, he reached out and boldly touched the fringe of freedom.

A Thread Is All You Need

You never wanted to be here, but here you are.

In the messiness of life, we can find ourselves at wits' end, and it's terrifying. It's not necessarily because of the circumstances we're facing as much as a lack of hope. Hopelessness is the by-product of messiness. It's as if we're free falling and we can't grab hold of anything, no position we can put ourselves in to brace our fall. We need a miracle.

Do you ever feel like Jesus simply passes you by on His way to work miracles in the lives of others? You're not alone. In Luke

8:40–48, a man named Jairus invites Jesus to come and heal his daughter, who is deathly ill. As Jesus is on His way to the man's home, He is passing through a crowd while the disciples try to make a way forward. In the crowd is a woman who suffers from an illness of her own. Jesus is on His way to heal someone else, but this woman sees the freedom available to her in Christ, and she boldly reaches out in faith and experiences freedom.

> Now when Jesus returned, the crowd welcomed him, for they were all waiting for him. And there came a man named Jairus, who was a ruler of the synagogue. And falling at Jesus' feet, he implored him to come to his house, for he had an only daughter, about twelve years of age, and she was dying.
>
> As Jesus went, the people pressed around him. And there was a woman who had had a discharge of blood for twelve years, and though she had spent all her living on physicians, she could not be healed by anyone.
>
> Luke 8:40–43 (ESV)

Twelve years. *Years.* I thought being sick for six months was brutal. This woman has been suffering for twelve years through this mess. Let me put that in context for you. Otherwise, we may skip over it as if it's just another crazy story in the Bible. At the time of me writing this, twelve years ago the iPhone didn't exist, Barack Obama hadn't announced his candidacy to run for president, the real estate market hadn't crashed, and the last installment of the Harry Potter series hadn't been released. For twelve years this woman has woken up in agony, only to look forward to falling asleep because it's the only peace she can find. Perhaps worse than the illness itself is that under Jewish law, a discharge of blood rendered you ceremonially unclean. Not only were you considered as unclean, but anyone who came into contact with you was also considered as unclean. Because this woman's condition is chronic and because she's a Jew, she can't participate in any religious or social gatherings. She may have even been excommunicated by her own family because of the severity of her condition and its effect on the people around her. She isn't allowed in the Temple or the synagogues, and nobody may touch her, or they will be considered as unclean. This woman is an exile.

Toward the end of verse 43, it looks as though the proverbial nail in the coffin seals the hopelessness of her circumstance. She's had an impossible time finding work or any way of making money with this illness, but with the little money she has to her name it tells us, "she had spent all her living on physicians, she could not be healed by anyone." Let's look at what this verse doesn't say before we look at what it does say. It doesn't say she had spent most of her living on physicians; it says she spent all of it. It doesn't say she was able to find a few helpful remedies from her local Walgreens to decrease her pain; it says she could not be healed by anyone. It doesn't say she had gone to see a physician; it says she had seen physicians—with an *s*. According to Mark 5:27 (ESV), "She had heard the reports about Jesus." She's heard about this man named Jesus and the miracles He has been performing, how He heals the sick and brings hope to the hopeless. Before the final nail can be struck in her coffin, she decides to go and see Him. She joins in the crowd as He is passing by, and she believes. If she can just reach out to Him in faith, it will change her life, so she interrupts Him. Some of you find yourselves in a similar position. Maybe your mess isn't obvious to many people, perhaps even most people around you who think they know you well. You've had a rough year, you feel enslaved to sin in your life, you've lost something, you've lost someone, you feel like an exile, you're facing a health crisis. Whatever it is, you're hanging on by a thread. But I would like to encourage you that if you're hanging on by a thread, a thread is all you need.

What Are You Holding On To?

If you haven't read or seen The Lord of the Rings trilogy, repent, then read and watch them.

Remember the powerful moment between Frodo and Sam in *The Two Towers*? They've just narrowly escaped death, managing to survive through a massive battle. They are separated from their friends and allies, many of their friends have turned their backs on them or been killed, they've been surrounded by complete and utter chaos for the better part of their journey, and the weariness is getting to Frodo. He wants to give up and go home, back to the good old days and simpler times.

Frodo says, "I can't do this, Sam."

"I know. It's all wrong. We shouldn't even be here. But we are. It's like in the great stories, Mr. Frodo. The ones that really mattered. Full of darkness and danger, they were. And sometimes you didn't want to know the end. Because how could the end be happy? How could the world go back to the way it was when so much bad had happened? But in the end, it's only a passing thing, this shadow. Even darkness must pass. A new day will come. And when the sun shines it will shine out the clearer. Those were the stories that stayed with you. That meant something, even if you were too small to understand why. But I think, Mr. Frodo, I do understand. I know now. Folk in those stories had lots of chances of turning back, only they didn't. They kept going. Because they were holding on to something."

"What are we holding on to, Sam?"

"That there's some good in this world, Mr. Frodo . . . and it's worth fighting for."[1]

When Frodo wants to give up hope, Sam wants to continue on. On the surface it looks like Sam is interrupting Frodo, but really it is an invitation to keep pressing forward in faith. He tells Frodo they are holding on to the idea that there is some good in the world that's worth fighting for. The woman in Luke 8, who has been ill for twelve years, is barely clinging to hope, but she's still hanging on. I believe that if we could ask this woman what she held on to, she would say, "Faith. That if I invite Jesus into my life, I will see the glory of God."

In Luke 8:44–46 it says that the woman "came up behind Jesus and touched the fringe of his garment, and immediately her discharge of blood ceased. And Jesus said, 'Who was it that touched me?' When all denied it, Peter said, 'Master, the crowds surround you and are pressing in on you!' But Jesus said, 'Someone touched me, for I perceive that power has gone out from me'" (ESV).

You have to appreciate Peter's sarcasm here. Jesus says, "Who was it that touched me?" Peter, looking at the huge crowd around them, pretty much says, "Oh, I don't know, Jesus. Maybe it was one of the hundreds of people within less than a foot of us! Why don't you tell us? You're the one who is God in the flesh!" But Peter doesn't understand what has happened and what is going to happen. Jesus doesn't ask because He doesn't know who touched Him. He asks because He is going to use the woman's pain as a platform to proclaim the power and goodness of God.

It's in the Walls

If you can find a couple of nickels to rub together, congratulations! You have as much money as Lindsey and I had on our wedding day. We didn't realize how poor we were until we started apartment hunting. The final complex we looked at was nestled away down a private road, right off the main artery that took Lindsey to school and work easily, and it allowed me to be at the church in five minutes. The location was perfect.

We toured the model and weren't appalled: two large rooms, two bathrooms, a living room, and a kitchen. The wood on the cabinets looked like it was straight out of 1973, the paint job was as bland as it gets, but we were young, and beggars can't be choosers. I went in to sign the contract and only made one specific request, a nonsmoking apartment, if they could help it. They told me that wouldn't be an issue, so I was confused when I opened the door to our new apartment for the first time and it smelled like someone had tried to re-create Woodstock.

Move-in day was a nightmare. Every time I went from unloading the truck outside to moving the furniture inside, it felt as if Babe Ruth were slugging me in the face with a baseball bat made of smoke. It reeked. Summer was in full swing too. Heat, sweat, and smoke filled the apartment while we hustled in and out. I went to the apartment complex office and asked them if they could try and reduce the smell. They tried to do a few things, but none of them worked. I went back and asked them if I could paint our place. At this point, they were getting frustrated with me, but when all your clothes smell like smoke because the smell is so bad, you tend to care less what they think. They told me that they had painted before we moved in and that I wasn't allowed to paint the apartment myself. Listen, I am somewhere in the neighborhood of 100 percent sure that they didn't paint our place before we moved in. I was ready to ask for forgiveness, not permission. My brother and I bought paint and covertly sneaked it into the apartment. Within three days we had the whole thing repainted. There were consequences, though. I think we lost ten years off our lifespan from the chemical inhalation. It was brutal, but happy wife, happy life, right?

On our first night back, it felt like we were living in a new apartment, without the smell of smoke. Lindsey was making dinner, so I decided to take a shower. As I stepped out of the shower and began drying myself off, the steam began to settle, and as it faded and my surroundings became clearer, I noticed something strange. Something was noticeably slithering down the white walls of the bathroom. It looked like a horror movie. Brown beads were rising to the surface and slowly streaking to the floor. If my walls were the coat of a tiger, the brown streaks were as many as its stripes. Reluctantly, I traced my finger along one of the streaks before it could make its way to the floor. Nicotine.

We had painted over every inch of that apartment. We covered up every previous blemish and mark on the walls. But we didn't eliminate the source of the problem; we merely covered up the symptoms with a superficial solution. We had mostly gotten rid of the smell, but there was still nicotine embedded in the walls. When it was exposed to the heat and a little steam from the shower, it came sweating through. The smell of smoke was symptomatic of a deeper problem. My superficial paint job couldn't get rid of a deeply rooted disease, but now it could be addressed since it had been brought to the surface.

"When the woman saw that she was not hidden, she came trembling, and falling down before Him, declared in the presence of all the people why she had touched Him, and how she had been immediately healed. And Jesus said to her, 'Daughter, your faith has made you well; go in peace'" (Luke 8:47–48 ESV). God will reveal what is hidden if it needs to be seen. It's hard to address something if it's hidden, but when you can see it, you can address it. This woman had an illness that wasn't easily fixed. No doctors were successful. In Mark 5:26 we're told "instead of getting better she grew worse." Jesus didn't call her out so He could figure out who had touched Him. This woman's illness went deeper than physicians could cure; they had given her superficial solutions to a complex problem. Jesus brought her illness to the surface, addressed it, and cleansed it. He called her out to cleanse her and call her what nobody else would—"daughter," deeply known, deeply loved, and completely healed.

Even If You Shake

What strikes me in Luke 8:47 is the brief mention of the woman's own self-awareness. "When she saw that she was not hidden, she came trembling." Think about this for a moment. This woman is not allowed to participate in religious or social outings. She has been excommunicated from her family and society. She has been hidden, living in isolation because of this mess for the past twelve years, but now she comes trembling. Why is she trembling? She is acknowledged for the first time in twelve years! She is seen. People have left her, distanced themselves from her, but Jesus calls out to her and draws near to her. She knows she isn't seen by a spouse, not by a boyfriend or girlfriend, not by a parent, or someone she admires; she is seen by God! Jesus brings her out of the shadows for all to see, and He evangelistically uses her pain as a platform to proclaim the good news of how she reached out to Him and was immediately healed, how her faith had made her well, and how God had worked in her life. My favorite part of this passage is in verse 44, when it says "touched the fringe of his garment." Many of us live with the mindset that unless we can grab a handful of Jesus's cloak, then our faith is too little to even try to reach out to Him. This woman touches a thread of Jesus's cloak and is immediately restored.

The beautiful thing about Jesus is that in your mess, He calls to you, draws near to you, and cleans you up. For twelve years this woman had been isolated and ostracized because people knew that if she touched them, they would be considered unclean. But when she reaches out to touch Jesus, it has the opposite effect. When she touches Him, the unclean doesn't contaminate the clean; the clean purifies the unclean.

Jesus is on His way to heal another man's daughter when this woman interrupts him. I think that for many of us, most of the time, we're content to let our circumstances keep us from coming to God because we feel as though we're being a burden to God. We don't want to interrupt Him. You've felt like you're on your own for a while now, so there's no point in going to God. You're used to the mess. You're used to watching Jesus pass you by on His way to work in the lives of other people. Let me say this, though, the only reason Jesus is on His way to heal that man's daughter is that Jesus was invited to do so.

Maybe you don't have an illness, and maybe you haven't been suffering for twelve years. Or maybe you are sick right now or you've been suffering through physical or emotional pain for even longer than twelve years. Maybe you've wasted your life savings trying to heal an illness. Maybe you've spent your life savings on temporary solutions to deeply rooted problems. What you've spent your life savings on—the paint job over the nicotine in your walls—may cover up some symptoms, but it doesn't touch the root of the issue. Maybe a wound in your life hasn't been able to be healed by anybody or anything, but you haven't invited the right person into your circumstance. This woman reaches out and touches the fringe of Jesus's garment, not to interrupt Him, but to invite the power of God in faith to do what nobody else could do—bring her freedom from her illness and isolation. You aren't being a burden to God by coming to Him with your mess. If there were ever a burden placed on God, it was the cross, but human interruption didn't cause the cross. The cross was God intervening in history as the ultimate invitation to be a part of His story. In Mark 5:28 the woman with this blood disorder says, "If I just touch his clothes, I will be healed." She couldn't have been more right.

Jesus doesn't only work in the lives of people who have the strength to run up to Him and grab hold of His cloak. If you're on your hands and knees, with enough faith to reach for a thread, then you have enough faith to interrupt Him with an invitation into your life and your circumstance. What you see as an interruption, God sees as an invitation to intervene for your good and His glory. Keep stepping toward Him, even if your knees shake. Jesus sees you. You aren't lost in the crowd. You are seen by God, and until that is enough, nothing else will be. If you're hanging on by a thread, be encouraged. A thread is all you need.

CHAPTER 7

The King of Thieves

Few things are more frustrating than feeling as though Jesus walks past you on His way to bless others. But it's important to remember, a feeling is just that, a *feeling*. Our feelings are misleading and easily manipulated if we're not vigilant. The more familiar you are with Jesus, the more you'll be able to recognize the truth: who you are in Him and how the enemy schemes against us. Of all the enemy's tactics, one cripples society today: comparison, the king of thieves.

It's been said before that comparison is the thief of joy. The first time I heard that saying, I wasn't sure if I agreed with the sentiment. In my eyes there were a lot of benefits to comparing myself with other people. Ephesians 5:1 (ESV) says, "Therefore be imitators of God," and in 1 Corinthians 11:1 (ESV), Paul says, "Be imitators of me, as I am of Christ." It looked as though Scripture supported comparison, that we need to look to the life of Paul and Jesus and strive toward that. But here's the thing: imitating isn't the same as comparing.

Imitation sees the admirable qualities in another and desires to implement them in our own lives for the betterment of ourselves in our walk with Christ. Comparison *envies* the qualities and things that someone else has and wants them for ourselves so that we can best those around us and turn our envy into their envy. It makes us feel as if our lives are worth less than others, or worse, worth more than others. The true issue lies between our ears.

The Enemy's Playground

Our mind is the enemy's playground. He can't create, but he can manipulate. He is adept at deception and a masterful manipulator of our thoughts. Comparison is the root of covetousness. Ever since the moment of the fall in Genesis 3, the enemy has not only tried but succeeded in manipulating us into believing lies. He didn't create the garden or anything in it, but he manipulated humanity's thoughts about God's ways, His creation, His word, and His promises, and it led to devastation.

> Now the serpent was more crafty than any of the wild animals the LORD God had made. He said to the woman, "Did God really say, 'You must not eat from any tree in the garden'?"
>
> The woman said to the serpent, "We may eat fruit from the trees in the garden, but God did say, 'You must not eat fruit from the tree that is in the middle of the garden, and you must not touch it, or you will die.'"
>
> "You will not certainly die," the serpent said to the

> woman. "For God knows that when you eat from it your eyes will be opened, and you will be like God, knowing good and evil."
>
> When the woman saw that the fruit of the tree was good for food and pleasing to the eye, and also desirable for gaining wisdom, she took some and ate it. She also gave some to her husband, who was with her, and he ate it.
>
> GENESIS 3:1–6

The enemy employs a number of strategies to throw us off the path God intends for us to follow. He tempts, lies, accuses, destroys, and misleads, to name a few. Do you see what he is doing here? He does all the above, but he gets Adam and Eve to compare where they are with where they could be. He says, Did God really say that? You won't die. Your eyes will be opened, and *you will be like God*. When they hear that they will be like God, they eat.

The more I thought about it and investigated my own life, I agree with the statement that comparison is the thief of joy. Not only is it the thief of joy; it's the king of thieves. It's the enemy's most effective tactic against people today. Because we are more connected than ever before, we are more susceptible to comparison than we've ever been. Every time we unlock our phones, we compare the messiness of our lives with the tidiness of others'.

The Most Dangerous Weapon in Human History Is in Your Hands

When I got my first phone, my plan had one hundred text messages and one hundred minutes for calls per month. I only had two numbers, Mom and Dad. You would have thought they gave me a nuclear weapon. My parents were acting as if they had handed me the most dangerous tool in history—they may have been on to something. I didn't get my first iPhone until I was in college. I can honestly say I'm thankful for that, but that didn't keep the comparison bug from biting me later in life. It's been a huge hindrance in my walk, seeing where others are, looking at where I am, and feeling insignificant.

Brian A. Primack, MD, PhD, and his colleagues at the University of Pittsburgh School of the Health Sciences analyzed 1,787 young adults, ages nineteen to thirty-two, to study depression and social media use and found that "multi-social media users are actually more likely to be depressed than their peers who are more social media conservative . . . [and] researchers determined that millennials who consistently used more than one platform for a long period of time—rather than only one social media platform—showed increased depression and anxiety."[1]

The American Academy of Pediatrics published an article on digital media, anxiety, and depression that said, "The representation of attractive people leading exciting and idealized lives in media programs invites social comparison and contributes to dissatisfaction with oneself. . . . Results indicated that technology-based social comparison and feedback seeking were associated with depressive symptoms that exceeded previous depressive symptom history. Adolescents may seek digital distraction from emerging anxiety or distress emotions, creating a reinforced behavioral avoidance of emotional experiences. Emotion regulation is an important skill that is developed in childhood and adolescence because individuals learn to handle and cope with strong emotions by experiencing them and developing internal regulatory processes."[2]

Is social media evil? Not at all. Like anything else, when consumed in moderation, it is a good thing and can be used for great purposes. The problem is that we are bingeing. Our addiction to social media is an epidemic unlike anything in the history of humanity. It's creating a space of unavoidable comparison that cultivates a callousness within us, and it's negatively affecting our self-esteem, health, and relationships with others, whether we know it or not.

We compare our messiness with others' beautifully organized aesthetic. But it goes even deeper than we realize. When we think of comparison, our minds immediately drift to the idea of seeing someone else's posts and wishing we could look as cool as they do—to have their style, travel to the places they travel, or be that photogenic. I wish the problem were only that superficial. The toxicity reaches further down, deep into the crevasses of our hearts. In my own life, I've caught Lindsey and me comparing our marriage to someone else's marriage, solely on the basis of what we see online. We've gone as far as arguing with each other over why our marriage looks so boring compared with the relationships of people who are complete strangers. I've seen people relaying what their devotional or study time looks like and found myself questioning whether my personal devotion to Jesus is on par with theirs, simply because of what I've seen as I scroll. What you see on social media is just a pretty filter on a broken image. We see the full collage of our mess and compare it with a touched-up photo of what others allow us to see. The enemy knows this, and he manipulates our thinking. It's easy to look at other people's lives through a screen and think they've got it all together. Don't buy into that, but most importantly, don't buy into the idea that what God is doing through someone else is taking away from what He's doing through you.

Run *Your* Race

I'm not big into horse racing, but I will catch some of the bigger races if I get the chance. If you're like me, you don't know many races off the top of your head, outside of the Kentucky Derby. I remember watching the Kentucky Derby years ago. I couldn't tell you who won because I was too busy trying to find out why the horses had covers over their eyes. At first the trainers led the horses into their little stable before setting them free to race around the track. I figured the flaps over their eyes helped keep them calm as they made their way into the stables. At some point before they were let loose, I thought someone would take the blinders off their eyes, but they didn't. The race began, and the blinders stayed on. I looked around confused: did no one else find this strange? I'll be the first to admit that I'm not the world's leading expert on horses, but it felt that as a general rule, being blind while moving that fast would not go well. I don't put a blindfold on when I drive, but maybe that's just me. My curiosity took over, and I had to look it up.

According to the Dallas Equestrian Center, "Horses sometimes need to be made to focus and blinders keep the horse's eye focused on what is ahead, rather than what is at the side or behind. That is why race horses are often given blinders—for the purpose of keeping them focused when racing round a racecourse. The jockey [the small guy on the horse] has little control over the horse. If a horse decides to take a different route, it will simply take the jockey with it, so this may pose problems. Troublesome race horses are fitted with blinders for their own safety and the jockey's safety."[3]

God is like the trainer. He's the One whom we have spent our time with privately, who knows us and we know Him, the One who has loved us, cared for us, and taught us how to run. No matter how hard the enemy tries to scream lies into our ears, it's the whispers of God that call us to the path we follow and the race we run. We're all just trying to run our race well on the path that God has placed us on.

The enemy is like the jockey. He has as much control as we're willing to give him. Sure, he may be on our back, and it appears as though he is the one in control, but he ultimately follows where we go. He can try to manipulate us into comparing ourselves to the horses beside us, but as long as we know the truth of God, we can block out the lies of the enemy.

We're like the horses. Sometimes our trainer has to put blinders on us so that we will stay focused on the race ahead, rather than what is happening around us. It can be frustrating. We want God to reveal everything to us, but if He didn't put the blinders on, we'd view our teammates as opponents. Our race isn't against them; it's with them. Sometimes they win; sometimes we win. But we don't run our race so that we can win; we do it so that the world knows He has already won.

The Message version of Psalm 119:1–3 says,

> You're blessed when you stay on course,
> walking steadily on the road revealed by God.
> You're blessed when you follow his directions,
> doing your best to find him.

That's right—you don't go off on your own;
you walk straight along the road he set.

The Luke Lezon translation of this verse? I'm glad you asked. "Stay. In. Your. Lane. *People*!" It's easier said than done. I would know. It's difficult to walk down the path that God has us on when we're constantly seeing the paths others are on. Comparing ourselves to other people is almost never fair on our end. We measure their strengths against our weaknesses, their highs against our lows, their joys against our sorrows.

We can't fully appreciate God's blessings in our lives if we're measuring them against the blessings in other people's lives. Keep your focus on the work God has given you, where He has you, and the work He has given you to do in this season. The work of the current season sets up the seasons to come. The grass isn't greener on the other side. You're just busy watching someone else water their yard while yours remains unattended. Seasons and circumstances are always changing. If you measure your value by temporary things, then you'll never understand your eternal value. Jesus didn't die so that you would wonder where your value lies; He rose so that you could know that it lives in Him.

An Original Work of Art

In the sixteenth century, Europe was in the sweet spot of the Renaissance. It was during the Renaissance that much of the architecture, paintings, and other pieces of art that we still celebrate were being created. The statue of *David,* the Sistine Chapel, the *Mona Lisa, The Last Supper,* were all being made by legendary artists like Michelangelo and Leonardo da Vinci. What a time to be alive! You could hardly brush your teeth, but you could use a paintbrush to make a masterpiece. These were strange times.

I doubt that amid all these famous artists many of you have heard of Raffaello Sanzio da Urbino, other than that he's the namesake of the best ninja turtle. His friends just called him Raphael, for obvious reasons. But he died early in life. Otherwise, we may have known him as well as some of the other artists. One article I read said, "Raphael is the supreme Renaissance painter, more versatile than Michelangelo, and more prolific than their older contemporary Leonardo."[4] Raphael was extremely gifted, equally talented as some of the greatest artists of all time, and his works were highly sought after.

Fast-forward to the nineteenth century. Former British Prime Minister George Hamilton-Gordon purchased a painting of the Virgin Mary, a painting he believed was an original work of Raphael's. Unfortunately, shortly after purchasing it, it was inspected and determined that it wasn't a genuine Raphael painting but probably just a copy of an inferior artist. So as time went by, there was seemingly nothing special about this painting, and in 1899 it was sold for twenty-five dollars. That's roughly $2,600 dollars by today's standards, if you're curious.[5]

Fast forward one more time with me to 2016. An art historian came across this painting and thought it had the characteristics of a textbook work of Raphael's. He heard that George Hamilton-Gordon had bought it thinking that it was a Raphael, so he asked to have it professionally cleaned and investigated. After examining it, they concluded that it was in fact a work of Raphael's. Not someone else's, not a copy, but an original work of art done by Raphael himself. This painting that was sold for twenty-five dollars is now estimated to be worth nearly twenty-six million dollars.

I tell you that story for this reason: your life, your story is more valuable than you think. Many of us think our story is just a copy. You look around you and see that somebody else looks as if they have a better version of what you have, or of what you wish you had, but you have gifts, talents, and abilities that God has given to you specifically. You are in possession of an original, but if you fail to recognize that, you will sell something priceless for pennies on the dollar compared with the riches of God's glory that are promised in Christ.

Don't compare who you are with who you aren't. You are uniquely and beautifully made. You bring something different to the kingdom than I do, and that's the beauty of it. Different people, from different backgrounds, with different gifts, working for the same King. That painting was worth infinitely more than it was originally valued at. Why? Because of whose the painting was, because of who created it.

The Cure for Comparison

We desperately need love and truth in the world today. Many people do things in the name of love; few people tell the truth. We need to be honest with ourselves before we can get to a point where we are satisfied with who we are in Christ, love who He has made us to be, and love those whom we compare ourselves with. The solution to our OCD (Obsessive Comparison Disorder) is a tough pill called humility. Comparison is the offspring of pride. It hurts to say that, because I know that this is true of me as well. Saint Augustine said, "It was pride that changed angels into devils; it is humility that makes men as angels."[6]

In his book *An All-Round Ministry: Addresses to Ministers and Students*, Charles Spurgeon says, "Let us not judge ourselves by others, and say, with deadening self-complacency, 'We are getting on well as compared with our brethren. There are not many additions to our churches, but we are as successful as others.' . . . Let us measure ourselves by our Master, and not by our fellow-servants: then pride will be impossible, but hopefulness will be natural."[7] In Spurgeon's statement you could switch the word "measure" with "compare," and it would have the same meaning. When we compare ourselves with our peers, it steals our joy, kills our calling, and pushes others down so we can stand on their shoulders as we try to satisfy our pride that desires so desperately to be seen. When we focus on imitating Christ, our only response is humility.

> Do nothing out of selfish ambition or vain conceit. Rather, in humility value others above yourselves, not looking to your own interests but each of you to the interests of the others.
>
> In your relationships with one another, have the same mindset as Christ Jesus:
>
> Who, being in very nature God,
> did not consider equality with God something to be used to his advantage;
> Rather, he made himself nothing
> by taking the very nature of a servant,
> being made in human likeness.

> And being found in appearance as a man,
> he humbled himself
> by becoming obedient to death—
> even death on a cross!
>
> PHILIPPIANS 2:3–8

It's much easier to subscribe to the world's view than the ways of Jesus. The devil doesn't present you with difficult choices; he presents you with easy ones. The only reason we say temptation is difficult is that our flesh and spirit are at war. If we were following the ways of the world and appeasing our flesh, life would be much simpler. The resistance is what makes it difficult. To follow Jesus is to follow His command in Matthew 16:24 (CSB), "If anyone wants to follow after me, let him deny himself, take up his cross, and follow me." To follow the world is the exact opposite. The world tells us to make our own names famous, soak up the spotlight, push others down to get ahead, leave people behind who stand in our way, and get rich or die trying. I often wonder how hard it would be to be in Jesus's shoes: for the devil to prowl, tempting me with all the kingdoms of the world, to know that heaven would answer at my call and save me from the cross but to carry out the will of the Father anyway. Philippians 2:9 says, "Therefore [because of His unfathomable display of humility all the way to the cross] God exalted him to the highest place and gave him the name that is above every name." Nobody has gone lower; nobody has been raised higher.

It's hard to throw stones if you're busy washing feet. We'd wash a lot more feet if we quit comparing and throwing stones at others, counting them as more significant than ourselves.

Comparison quickly turns into competition. We want a leg up on the people around us. It's an unhealthy way to try and mask our insecurities and feelings of inferiority. Your success won't look the same as others', and that's okay. We need each other. This journey is hard, the path is treacherous, and we can't endure it alone. We need to encourage and be encouraged. This is about His glory, not ours. Pride compares ourselves with others; humility finds contentment with who we are in Christ. How low do we need to get? Low enough to wash each other's feet. If someone else's feet are dirty, it doesn't make ours any cleaner. When I think about how Jesus hung on a cross for us when we could do nothing for Him, how He sees our sin so clearly, yet loves us so much, I can only conclude that imitating His life and embracing humility is a much better way than comparing my life to others' and lashing out in pride. When you find yourself comparing yourself to others, remember this—nothing they are doing and nothing that they have will ever be a better replacement for what Jesus has done for you, who He is to you, and who He has made *you* to be.

Who Told You That?

After Adam and Eve sinned, Genesis 3:8–9 tells us that they "heard the sound of the Lord God as he was walking in the garden in the cool of the day, and they hid from the Lord God among the trees of the garden. But the Lord God called to the man, 'Where are you?'"

From the beginning of time, the enemy has been trying to convince us that God isn't enough, that God is withholding something that would be enough to appease our appetite for validation. That's what comparison is, isn't it? We desire something someone else has. We're dissatisfied with God, with what He has given us, with where He has us, and we are convinced that if we just had what *they* have, then it would be better. That's how the enemy deceived Adam and Eve. He got them to compare what God had given them with what they could have, and he lied about the effect it would have. He insisted that walking with God wasn't enough. If they ate from the tree, they wouldn't just walk with God; they would be gods. The result of eating the fruit? They hid. Guilt and shame had entered their hearts because of their disobedience. The enemy successfully manipulated them into a game of comparison. The enemy will coax you into comparison when you start to believe the lie that God isn't enough, and if you play the game, you lose. Every time.

God calls to them, *"Where are you?"* His question was greater than a desire to pinpoint their position; He knew where they were. God's question is really an answer to a question humanity has always asked: does God see my mess? Does He still care about me and love me despite my mishaps? Yes, He does. From the moment Adam and Eve disobeyed God and hid from Him in the garden of Eden, He has lovingly pursued us.

In Matthew 16:15 Jesus asks the disciples a similar yet different question, "Who do you say I am?" It's the impulsive Peter who pipes up, "You are the Messiah, the Son of the living God" (v. 16). When Peter declares this, Jesus blesses him. Why? Because he nailed it. If Peter's declaration was true, if Jesus is the Messiah, the Christ, the Son of the living God, then Jesus is *enough.* There is nothing else to strive for; salvation is here. The once-and-for-all atoning sacrifice of Jesus, the perfect, blameless, innocent Lamb, was about to die a death that justifies us. His blood washes away our messes and makes us clean. What failed in the garden of Eden was about to be redeemed in the garden of Gethsemane.

Genesis 3:10–11 says, "He answered, 'I heard you in the garden, and I was afraid because I was naked; so I hid.' And [God] said, 'Who told you that you were naked?'" Jesus didn't die so you would wonder whether you're enough; He died so you could walk in the freedom of knowing that you are fully known and fully loved. When you compare yourself with others and wonder whether you're successful enough, pretty enough, fit enough, funny enough, entertaining enough, or whatever it is, you are operating outside of God's original intent. God asks Adam and Eve, "Who told you that you were naked?" They were never supposed to feel that awkwardness, that guilt and shame. So let me ask you, Who told you that you're not enough? Who told you that you need to look at someone else's life and measure yourself against them? To desire what they have as if that would solve a Savior-sized need in your life?

There is nothing somebody else has that will satisfy your desire for more. Only one well will quench your thirst. If you have Jesus, you have everything you need. No comparison needed.

Your mess is worth infinitely more than you could ever imagine. If your calling is to fly but you're focused on how well others swim, you'll always see yourself as less than. Keep your mind set on Christ. Jesus sees what you can't see in yourself. Walk with Him, run with Him, and rest in Him. Don't sell yourself short on what God has paid so much for. You are loved. No filter required.

CHAPTER 8

Burn through the Night

You hate the feeling, but you can't shake it.

No matter how the enemy attacks us, it's important we fight back. The fight means we're alive. We know that God fights with us, that He goes before us and has made a way, a path to victory through His Son, Jesus. We are strengthened by His grace, suited for battle with the armor of God, but sometimes we find ourselves in dark places.

When Apathy Attacks

I'll often sit down with someone who is struggling in their faith, and they'll tell me they're upset with God, even furious at Him, but that doesn't bother me. That means they care, that they can acknowledge God is there. Even if they're somewhat distant because they're frustrated with God, they're asking the right questions. I only get frustrated with people that I care about. I get frustrated with my parents, my brother, my wife, my friends. I don't usually get upset with strangers. I may not like the way some strangers behave or love the way they carry themselves, but I find it much more difficult to be upset or frustrated by them than by people I know well. I must deposit something into the bank of a relationship for me to withdraw anything substantial, joy or anger. I'll tell you what really scares me when I sit down with someone to discuss where they're at in their relationship with God—indifference.

Elie Wiesel was a winner of the Nobel Peace Prize, author, activist, and Holocaust survivor. He wrote and spoke often about the horrors of his experiences in concentration camps during the Holocaust, and he said this, "The opposite of love is not hate, it's indifference. The opposite of art is not ugliness, it's indifference. The opposite of faith is not heresy, it's indifference. And the opposite of life is not death, it's indifference."[1] One of the great opponents of faith is an adversary called apathy. Apathy is defined as a "lack of interest, enthusiasm, or concern."[2] Have you looked at the messiness of your life and found moments, perhaps seasons, where you've lost enthusiasm in the pursuit of knowing God and making God known? Has reading Scripture ever felt like an assignment more than joyful fulfillment? Has prayer ever felt like a burden, more of an exercise where you try to stay awake instead of a necessity? *It's okay if you feel that way, but it's not okay to stay that way.*

Psalm 63:1 says,

> You, God, are my God,
>   earnestly I seek you;

I thirst for you,
　　my whole being longs for you,
in a dry and parched land
　　　　where there is no water.

Isn't that beautiful? But as picturesque and eloquent as this psalm is, I have to be honest. I've often felt unproductively content with where I'm at, indifferent to the idea of doing anything more than I've already done. I don't always earnestly seek God, and I don't always feel like God will satisfy the thirst of my soul. That's where the fight occurs, in the field between love and indifference. It's a battle we all end up fighting. To feel apathetic is to be human. At one time or another, we feel indifferent toward nearly everything in our lives. We feel apathetic in our work, toward our children, our marriage, school, friendships, and even our faith. Many of you probably feel this way now. If you don't, then you either have felt this way before or you will in the future.

When we feel spiritually dry, it's typically because of some mess we're in or sin we're stuck in. It drains the passion in our relationship with God, a passion that used to fuel us. We feel as if we're sliding down a hill, when we were previously leaping and bounding over mountains. If you aren't aggressive in your resistance of apathy, apathy won't only be a result of the messiness of your life; it will turn into the biggest mess in your life. But let me say this: you don't have to try to justify why you're feeling apathetic. It happens.

Apathy is like carbon monoxide: it's colorless, tasteless, and odorless. It causes symptoms like weakness and confusion. That's how you know it's present, but by that time it could be too late. You need to set up an alarm in your home to detect it. Otherwise, it may sneak up on you and kill you if you don't react. The same goes for apathy in our faith. We have to fight for faith, otherwise apathy will take it from us. So how do we retrieve and maintain that passion in our pursuit of God? Well, the first step is to stop using gasoline.

Bachelor Parties and Blowing Things Up

My bachelor party was probably one of the most testosterone-driven bachelor parties in the history of bachelor parties. Not in the crazy, stereotypical way, but in every man's inner pyrotechnic kind of way. I will never forget it.

Everything started off casual and low-key. We decided to have a fire that night, so we put gasoline on the wood, lit it, and exchanged embarrassing stories about my past and some moments of sheer stupidity. One of the guys found an old can of spray paint, threw it in the fire when nobody was looking, and all of a sudden, *boom*! The bang reverberated through the night sky, bits of fire and embers shot out in all directions, and for a moment it felt as though the world had come to a halt.

Cautiously, we all looked up at the fire. We had all ducked and fallen into the fetal position. After the exchange of a few glances, a new change of underwear, and coming to the realization that we were all still alive, we lost our minds. We started screaming, chest bumping, and freaking out about how amazing that was. You would think we had just discovered fire. I can't tell you what it is exactly with men, fire, and destruction, but it's as though we come alive as we walk the line of idiocy and consequence. After the explosion, we had withdrawals. We didn't just want more; we *needed* more.

The next thing we knew, one of the guys drove down to the fire, a few of us piled into his truck, and we headed to Lowe's. I ran in there and a found a sweet old lady working and said, "Ma'am, I need all your spray paint cans."

"Ok, son. Follow me. I'll show you where we keep those." We walked to the paint section of the store, then made our way down the aisle where they had cans of spray paint. She grabbed a flat of them and handed them to me.

I pulled a Ron Swanson and said, "Ma'am, I think there has been some sort of miscommunication here. I think what you thought I said was that we need *some* of your spray paint cans, but what I actually said was that we need *all* of your spray paint cans."

We emptied our wallets, loaded Lowe's entire inventory of spray paint into the back of the truck, and headed back down to the fire. We threw cans in the fire and laughed like madmen as they exploded. Then somebody got really creative. There was an old pellet gun in the house that someone had discovered while the rest of us depleted the stock of spray paint. They set one of the cans near the fire, shot it, and the explosion was even crazier. At this point, we were all laughing maniacally, and if anyone were to have mistakenly shown up to our fire, they would have thought there was some cultish ritual taking place.

Eventually, our fun ended. We were out of spray paint, and we knew Lowe's was out of spray paint, so we grabbed some gasoline to see how high we could get the flames to go. Like I said, walking that fine line between idiocy and consequence. We found a good amount of gasoline, but it didn't take long before we were out. When that was gone, our compulsion to see objects combust could no longer be satisfied. The fire died, and we went inside. There was nothing to see anymore, nothing to get excited about. When morning came, I got up early to clean up the yard. You may have thought a spray paint civil war had been fought the night before, because the yard looked like a nineties tie-dye shirt. After I got all the cans, I went over to look at the fire. It was only ash around some larger pieces of wood that hardly looked like they had burned. The gasoline had simply become a coating around some of the pieces, and when the gasoline burned off, the fire died. It was a superficial burn that didn't last through the night. Not only did the fire not last through the night, but it hardly lasted a few minutes. It created an incredible show, but only for a moment.

We become indifferent in our faith when we run out of gasoline. If you've experienced moments of spiritual indifference, then you've probably experienced moments of spiritual high, those moments when you feel overly zealous for the things of God and feel as if there is nothing else in the world. It's like starting a fire with gasoline. For a brief moment, the brightness is spectacular, the warmth envelops you, the flames rise above the trees as they reach for the heavens, but just as quickly as it burst onto the scene, it's gone.

Kindling vs. Gasoline

In Isaiah 51, Isaiah is preaching to people who look around them and see devastation. During this period in history, the writer of Isaiah appears to be addressing the captives of ancient Israel that were exiled to Babylon under the reign of King Nebuchadnezzar. While exiled, they are desperate to return home. They want to live the life they once knew. One that flourished. They had

had agricultural successes and an ever-growing city that teemed with life and prosperity, their beautiful city of Jerusalem. When the Israelites were finally able to return, it wasn't what they remembered. Jerusalem had been destroyed, the land was desolate, the temple had to be rebuilt, crops had to be regrown, and rubble had to be swept away. It was a mess. They had to start over. It'd be easy to allow apathy to settle in. They were exiled for seventy years in a foreign land, only to come home to dashed hopes and dreams. If you and I were Israelites returning from Babylonian captivity, we'd probably feel indifferent to hope.

Maybe that is you—you're in a place right now where you feel indifferent to hope. You don't know how you got to this point, but you look around at your life and all you see is dashed hopes and dreams, rubble and devastation, a mess that will take an inordinate amount of work. These words from Isaiah are jumper cables for faith; they breathe passion into an indifferent heart. They're the alarm that warns you about the carbon monoxide in your home, but they're also the instructions on how to get out of there and get to safety.

Isaiah 51:1 says, "Listen to me, you who pursue righteousness and who seek the LORD." The Israelites have a history of having a hearing problem. So do we. Here God speaks through Isaiah to His people, saying, Listen up! Pursue righteousness, seek the Lord. God is calling on His people to start their way back to faith in the smallest of ways, by listening to His voice, to pursue and seek Him. Do you see how countercultural that is? We desperately crave the explosion. Where are the spray paint cans, pellet guns, and gasoline?

Faith that is struggling and faith that is flourishing both swing on the hinge of simplicity. When my faith is driest, the last thing I need to do is step on a stage and preach. I need to sit down and pray. In my own very unofficial case study of discussions with friends, there is a commonality between those who are feeling spiritually dry and those ablaze. Those who are spiritually dry are failing to do the little things, such as opening God's Word or communing with Him in prayer regularly, but those who are spiritually on fire are consistently doing those things. You may think, is that it? That seems too simple. Well, you're not wrong. But I would remind you of this: eating and drinking seem simple, but if you fail to do them, you will feel frail and exhausted, or worse.

Isaiah is telling them to start with kindling. With kindling, you take your time picking up the seemingly easy and simple things—small, dry twigs and sticks. Once they catch fire, you methodically add larger pieces. You can leave the fire all night, and in the morning the embers will still be burning. Kindling isn't as sexy as gasoline. It doesn't create the show that draws attention, but it lasts. People show up to throw gasoline on the fire, but when the gas can is empty, the show is over. Kindling doesn't just start fires; it sustains them. One night it creates a large bonfire, and though it may lose its roaring flame, the embers remain.

We've become desensitized to the miracle of fire itself. If the flames don't dance, we don't care. We don't want to take the time to create embers, because we've seen what gasoline can do. But we also know what it can't do. It can't sustain. My question to you is this: what are you using to start the fire?

Isaiah 51 continues in verses 1 and 2,

> Look to the rock from which you were cut
> and to the quarry from which you were hewn;

look to Abraham, your father,
and to Sarah, who gave you birth.
When I called him he was only one man,
and I blessed him and made him many.

Isaiah admonishes the people to look at God's work through people of faith in the past. Abraham and Sarah weren't working with gasoline. Abraham started as one man, and his wife, Sarah, was barren, but Abraham faithfully gathered the kindling, and God multiplied his efforts. God works spectacularly in the unspectacular. We can look at God's faithfulness in the past, in the lives of others, and know that it is a promise of the potential for future blessing.

Romans 4:18–21 gives beautiful insight into the value of kindling: "Against all hope, Abraham in hope believed and so became the father of many nations, just as it had been said to him, 'So shall your offspring be.' Without weakening in his faith, he faced the truth that his body was as good as dead—since he was about a hundred years old—and that Sarah's womb was also dead. Yet he did not waver through unbelief regarding the promise of God, but was strengthened in his faith and gave glory to God, being fully persuaded that God had power to do what he had promised."

Abraham's body was as good as dead, and Sarah's womb was dead, but Abraham believed in God's promise. He didn't believe it when the promise was in sight but when it seemed insane. God didn't give Abraham gasoline; He told him to start picking up kindling.

A lot of our issues with apathy stem from using gasoline. We've gone to the conferences, experienced spiritual highs with the expectation that they will last, only for normalcy to take its toll when we get home. We've had weeks when we feel as though we are seeing God meeting our needs and blessing us abundantly, only to get to the next week and feel as if our passion for Him has begun to unravel. New needs go unmet, and we get bored with our blessings and look to new ones. We've had moments when we've seen the effects of gasoline. We've seen the fire burn bright and the flames reach high, but when they're gone, we think something is off with our faith or with God, when really, it's our method that's off. We think, "God, I've seen You do the spectacular! Why am I not seeing flames reach the heavens day in and day out? Why aren't You here now like You were then?" We're like the Israelites saying, "God I dream of a Jerusalem that flourished. I remember the vineyards and the vegetation. I remember the beauty and the life in the city, and now all I see is devastation and smoldering embers of something that was once spectacular!" But what they forgot and what we're forgetting is that embers are the bedrock of bonfires. Embers are not the absence of God's warmth; they're the steadfastness of it.

Abraham lived many years before being multiplied. He picked up kindling for a lifetime before God multiplied him, but we tend to only remember the greatness of God's work through Abraham. We remember the miracle of Abraham's multiplication, but we don't talk nearly as much about Abraham's dedication. It's like Isaiah 51 says, Abraham sought the Lord and pursued righteousness. He was just one when God called him. Against all hope, in hope, Abraham believed. He pursued righteousness. Romans 4:22 says, "This is why 'it was credited to him as righteousness.'" Isaiah 51:2 reminds those who pursue righteousness that God blesses and multiplies. It didn't come without painstaking work and waiting, though. When the messiness of life invites apathy to attack, remember, against all hope—believe in hope, the hope we have in Jesus.

Suicidal Thoughts and Sibling Love

Obsessive Compulsive Disorder (OCD) runs in my family. It's not your typical person's "I'm so OCD about _____" comment but the real deal. OCD doesn't only mean you wash your hands thirty-five times a day or have to have things organized. Some situations are like that, but that's a lazy stereotype. OCD is a relentless attack on the mind. My dad and I struggle with it, and it's exhausting, but my younger brother, Alex, has waged war against it since he was diagnosed as a boy. Like any war, it has at times been life-threatening. By the grace of God, Alex and I are now inseparable, but it wasn't always like that.

When we were growing up, my brother and I weren't close. Apathetic is how I would describe our relationship at that time. I was constantly on the go, out with friends, at a party, playing basketball, on the lake, something. Alex never was, and I thought that was strange. In addition to looking nothing alike, our personalities couldn't be more different. I'm a social butterfly; Alex is extremely introverted. Not until later did I come to understand why that is and how difficult it is to grow up with OCD. I knew Alex had OCD, but I was indifferent to what that meant. I thought it was an excuse to have strange tendencies in which he seemed to draw attention to himself. I never asked him about it, and I never even really asked my parents much about it. This is all terribly embarrassing to admit, but I just didn't care, at least I thought I didn't.

I remember it being a hot, sunny Dallas summer day in the great country of Texas. I was a junior in high school, Alex was a freshman, and both of my parents were working. I called my mom and told her about my plans to hang out with friends. She didn't say anything directly, but she kept alluding to the idea of me staying home. I could tell she didn't want to upset me, but it felt as if she was hiding something.

"Why do you want me to stay home so bad?"

"I just think you should hang with Alex."

"Why do you guys treat him like he is five? I'm not going to stay at the house and babysit Alex." My mom started sobbing.

"Why are you crying?"

She composed herself just long enough to get the words out before breaking down again, "Luke, you need to stay home because Alex isn't safe at home by himself. He might hurt himself."

"What?" I was dumbfounded. "What do you mean hurt himself? Like suicidal?"

"Yes," she wept, "I don't think he would actually do it, but I don't want to find out." Things felt as though they had broken apart but also fallen together at the same time. I had no idea that this mess existed in our home. That apathy in my relationship with Alex was exchanged for action. I had to say something, do something. After I got off the phone, I didn't move for a second. I finally walked to the kitchen and got a glass of water. My mouth was dry. My head felt empty. Alex walked out of his room.

"Hey," I said, staring a hole through him, unsure how to start this conversation.

"Hey." He gave me a confused look. He knew something was up.

I just lost it. I cried and panicked at the same time, hyperventilating, catching my breath to let the sobs flow and utter a few words at a time, "Mom said . . . well she just told me . . . would you really hurt yourself? You wouldn't? Right . . . ? You can't . . . I couldn't handle it. I . . . I love you . . . please don't . . . you can't . . . because I can't." He looked at me sternly but with a softness I'd never seen before. We both hadn't been here before. I put my hands over my face, weeping.

He hugged me and whispered, "I won't. I love you too."

Apathy is a powerful adversary, but it is no match for love.

Give and Take

Isaiah gives the apathetic heart a reason to get up in the morning when he says this in Isaiah 51:3:

> The Lord will surely comfort Zion
> and will look with compassion on all her ruins;
> he will make her deserts like Eden,
> her wastelands like the garden of the Lord.
> Joy and gladness will be found in her,
> thanksgiving and the sound of singing.

These words are the smell of coffee being poured before the sun comes up. Isaiah is giving us insight into one of the many characteristics of who God is, that because God is a loving God, He is also the God of exchange. He exchanges our discouraged places of waste for comfort. He exchanges a night in the wilderness for a morning stroll through Eden. He exchanges our deserts for the garden of the Lord. Where we wallow in despair, joy and gladness will be found. Where our voices have gone hoarse from the screaming and sobbing, we will rejoice in thanksgiving and a voice of song.

Abraham and Sarah couldn't have children. It was a waste place in their lives, a wilderness that seemingly had no promise of producing anything. The Israelites returned to their homeland from captivity, a land they dreamed of while in exile, and as they looked over the land, it had been laid to waste, now a desert of desolation. Maybe that's you as you look at the landscape of your own life. Apathy has made its home in your heart. You feel as if everyone else has a bonfire, while you're working with a few embers. You feel like Abraham and Sarah: your life is barren, and you're trying to garden in the desert. Nothing is working out the way you had hoped, and now you're indifferent to everything in general, including your relationship with God. It feels like there is no reason for hope, but if you're in Christ, you don't live life for hope, you live life in hope. It's unshakable.

Apathy is often the by-product of unrealistic expectations. You won't keep a fire blazing with gasoline. It takes the monotony of searching for kindling. It takes the tedious care of protecting a small flame, carefully breathing oxygen into it so it burns brighter and faster. Your faith is stronger than you believe it to be; you're simply unhappy with what you see. I'm not telling you to lower your expectations. I'm telling you that you've had low expectations. I want your fire to last through the night, not burn bright for just a moment.

As you go through life and scroll through your feeds,

everyone is documenting their fire, right? We're all trying to distract others from the messiness in our lives by trying to convince the world that our fire is more spectacular than it really is. You see that you only have embers, while others have bonfires. But it isn't about the height of the flames; it's about the quality of the kindling. I've got a lot of cool photos of the fire the night of my bachelor party when we poured gasoline on the fire. I didn't take any photos of how dead our fire was five minutes later or the mess I had to pick up the next day. But Scripture doesn't crown the one who is the fastest or burns the brightest, but the one who endures the length of the race, the one who has the endurance to burn through the night. Hebrews 10:36 (ESV) says, "You have need of endurance, so that when you have done the will of God you may receive what is promised."

It's Time to Catch Fire Again

So what do you do? You hate these apathetic feelings, but you're having a difficult time shaking them. I'll tell you what I do. I put my pride aside and take the focus off myself. When I've gotten used to the fun of gasoline, it's typically because I'm trying to satisfy my own desire to see something spectacular. Don't get it twisted, though. Embers are spectacular. The spectacular isn't in the size of the show but the longevity of it, which is why I rewire my focus from my desire for Christ, to Christ's desire for me. I set my eyes on His love for me, His compassion for me that has never failed. Our feelings toward God don't change His feelings toward us. We didn't work our way to God; He worked His way to us. Jesus made a way to faith that we couldn't make for ourselves. Apathy isn't a reason to give in but to dig in. Dig your heels into the dirt and stand firm on the foundation of Jesus Christ. If you feel spiritually dry, be encouraged—dry things catch fire quickly. It only takes a spark. All you need is good kindling. Find the pieces that ignite your faith, light the fire, and protect the embers. Go ahead—burn through the night.

CHAPTER 9

From Mess to Masterpiece

The Renaissance produced some of the most famous artists and works of art of all time: Leonardo da Vinci, Michelangelo, the *Mona Lisa, The Last Supper,* the Sistine Chapel, and many more. But few are more well-known than Michelangelo's *David.* Giorgio Vasari, who wrote a biography on Michelangelo, said this about *David,* "When all was finished, it cannot be denied that this work has carried off the palm from all other statues, modern or ancient, Greek or Latin; no other artwork is equal to it in any respect, with such just proportion, beauty and excellence did Michelangelo finish it."[1] When *David* was complete and shown to the members of the board who had commissioned the sculpture, they described it as, "far too perfect," but it wasn't always that way.

Inconvenience in the Courtyard

Twenty-six-year-old Michelangelo began working on the marble block that would eventually become *David* in 1501, but he wasn't the first artist to work on this particular block of marble. In 1464 work on the marble began, but the original artist never finished it. In 1475 another artist began working on the same block, but he too could never create anything from it. The two artists both cited the same issue with the marble: it had too many imperfections and was too messy of a project to carry out. After being rejected twice, the block sat in an open courtyard for decades. It would be nearly forty years before Michelangelo accepted the challenge of working with the marble.

The work that Michelangelo put into *David* is the stuff of legends. Michelangelo worked in secret in the courtyard. He worked in the pouring rain in sopping wet clothes. He didn't eat much, and he slept very little. When he did sleep, he would often lie down next to the statue, fully clothed, working at random and at all hours of the night. Three years later, in 1504, *David* was finished. The details of his anatomy blew spectators away. The veins in his hands, the soul in his eyes, the curls in his hair, the muscles flexed in his thigh—Michelangelo had made a masterpiece.

David's story started off like many of ours—rough. He spent some time with the wrong crowd, had relationships with a few artists where things didn't go well. He was abandoned, and nobody wanted him. Who would want to invest in something that was riddled with imperfections and flaws? He was too big to throw away and too ugly to be made beautiful. What changed? One of the greatest artists of all time got his hands on that mess and turned it into a masterpiece. He grabbed his mallet and chisel and went to work. The way this unwanted, oversized block of marble went from mess to masterpiece had nothing to do with the block itself. Michelangelo could have carved *David* from any other block and it would have been beautiful, but could any other artist have carved *David*? I don't think so.

God doesn't need much. Your greatest ability is availability. If you want to be what Ephesians 2:10 (NLT) calls "God's masterpiece," you don't have to come to Him with certain levels of talent or ability; you simply need to come to Him. Surrender yourself to Him. I can't be who God is creating me to be if I only surrender parts of me. I have to hand over everything, even what I may see as imperfections or parts of my life that I would prefer to remain untouched. What God creates isn't common. He is in the business of sculpting *David*s. When it looks like no more moves can be made, that's precisely when God moves the most. In the seemingly impossible, God's glory shines.

Today you can still see the statue of *David* in Florence, Italy, where millions of people visit it each year, but there was a period of time when David was merely a massive slab of marble, and not just a slab of marble—but one that was considered worthless. Millions of people who visit the masterpiece each year may know nothing about the story of the mess it once was. You know what's interesting, though? The mess doesn't detract from *David*'s story; it attracts us. I enjoy art, and the Renaissance fascinates me. I read up on this story in college, and it has always stuck with me. I've shared this story of *David* on countless occasions. When I tell people about it, I get the same response: a deeper appreciation for the work of art that it is today. Ironically, in our own lives, it's the exact opposite.

We don't want to share the messy parts of our stories. We have this preconceived notion that if we do, people will look down on us and think less of us. But that's the issue: too much focus on us. The fulcrum of our story isn't about how gross our mess was, but how glorious the Artist is. That's where everything turns around. Yes, the messiness in our lives is nothing we're proud of, but it's certainly nothing to be ashamed of either. God took away our shame and clothed us in righteousness, the same way Michelangelo chiseled away *David*'s flaws and sculpted him into something beautiful. We know what kind of mess David was, and because of that, the masterpiece *David* became isn't a testament to how amazing he is; it's a testament to how masterful Michelangelo was. We were a mess, and we still have messes in our lives, but God chose our block, even with its flaws, and He is still sculpting us—from a mess to a masterpiece.

The League of Shadows

First Kings 6 is a chunk of Scripture we are probably tempted to skip over. In Israel's history, they had spent a fair amount of time wandering and being on the move. To match their nomadic circumstances, they originally created a portable tabernacle, where God's presence could dwell among His people. After entering the Promised Land, they didn't need a portable tabernacle. They could now build a permanent temple in Jerusalem. That's what we read in 1 Kings 6, a description of the making of the first temple.

I'll let you read it for yourself, but allow me to point out one verse that sticks out. In verse 7 it says, "In building the temple, only blocks dressed at the quarry were used, and no hammer, chisel or any other iron tool was heard at the temple site while it was being built." If you keep reading, the description continues, but there is something eye-opening about verse 7. It interjects with critical insight about the materials that were used to create the temple. It tells us where they were prepared and why they were prepared. Solomon has his many reasons for doing this, but there is something we can learn here. The stones were prepared at a different site than the actual construction site of the temple. This was done so that the construction site of the temple was quiet, orderly, and efficient.

God does this with us. He pulls us aside to the secret place, a quiet place, away from the noise and distractions. He keeps the promotion we want just out of reach so that our motivations are focused on building His kingdom and not our own. Do we want the promotion to help others and bring glory to God? Or to help stack our savings? He doesn't put us in a position to be the leader immediately, because a leader who leads simply to elevate themselves is not a leader; they're a parasite. With good reasons, God waits to give, or will entirely withhold, what we desperately desire. He molds men and women in their character and motives by keeping them outside their fleshly desires and inside of His glorious will. He doesn't do this to punish us but to prepare us for His purposes. David was unaware that his brothers were lining up to see who would be anointed as the next king of Israel. He was tucked away in the field, shepherding the sheep. Even after he was anointed, he didn't become king for over a decade. It is in those seemingly insignificant moments that the truly significant things happen. It's where the mess becomes the masterpiece. Michelangelo molded *David* in secret. Solomon prepared the stone for the temple at a secret construction site. Jesus was taken into the wilderness before He launched His ministry. He would go to the quiet places to pray.

We live in a culture that is desperate to be noticed by anyone and everyone. We are drawn to the noise. Don't detest those moments that go unseen. Being seen does not equate to being significant. God sculpts *David*s in the shadows. He prepares the stones with His hammer and chisel in the shadows of the quarry, because if you're not prepared to be who God has called you to be in the shadows, you will shrivel in the spotlight. Shadows get a bad rap. They're gloomy and dark. Here's the thing: I'm from Dallas, Texas. It's a fight to find a shaded parking spot. Shadows don't always represent dark and gloom; sometimes they are the relief we so desperately need.

Psalm 91:1 (CSB) says, "The one who lives under the protection of the Most High dwells in the shadow of the Almighty." In the presence of God, shadows aren't an enemy but an ally. They are the evidence of His protection and care for us. German playwright Johann Wolfgang von Goethe wrote this line into one of his plays, "There is a strong shadow where there is much light."[2] The light of Christ shines in us and through us, but when needed, shadows are used to protect us and bring us back to those moments of molding, to find the relief in the shadows that we so desperately need to become who God intended.

In *The Dark Knight Rises*, Batman and Bane are in the middle of an epic battle. As Batman realizes that he is being outdueled, he uses one of his slick gadgets to turn off the lights. Bane's response is incredible: "Ah, you think darkness is your ally? You merely adopted the dark. I was born in it, molded by it. I didn't see the light until I was already a man, by then it was nothing to me but blinding! The shadows betray you, because they belong to me."[3]

I think Bane's quote represents the way we need to look at the shadows. Most people are too quick to associate shadows with the enemy. Shadows don't belong to the enemy. The shadows belong to whomever and whatever is casting them. When you live under the protection of the Most High and dwell in the shadow of the Almighty, it is there that God does some of His most significant molding and shaping. I'm not afraid of the shadows. I'm being shaped in private under the shadow of my Father's protection. Not everyone needs to know the plans God has prepared for you. Shadow seasons are sculpting seasons. By the time I recognized that people strive for significance by chasing the spotlight, I saw how blinding it could be. I knew who God made me to be in the shadows and that wouldn't be changed by the lights. According to Colossians 1:16 (ESV), "By him all things were created, in heaven and on earth, visible and invisible, whether thrones or dominions or rulers or authorities—all things were created through him and for him." By Him, through Him, and for Him all things were created. Everything belongs to Jesus; even the shadows are His. The enemy thinks the shadows are his ally? No, I was molded there, shaped there, prepared there. I belong to Christ, and who I've become is used to house His glory.

Take Your Place

Stones have their dings and unique characteristics; none is exactly like the other. That is part of what makes the church so beautiful. Many different people (stones) come together for something bigger than themselves. Made in the shadows, with their personal dings and dysfunctions, God has made a place for them. He has prepared them. Not a single stone that has been put into the hands of God is too messed up to be used for His purposes, not even yours.

As Christians who believe that Jesus, the Son of God, lived the perfect life we couldn't and died the death we deserved, was crucified, buried, raised, and sits on the throne of heaven, we make up a different temple, a living temple. Ephesians 2:19–22 says, "You are no longer foreigners and strangers, but fellow citizens with God's people and also members of his household, built on the foundation of the apostles and prophets, with Christ Jesus himself as the chief cornerstone. In him the whole building is joined together and rises to become a holy temple in the Lord. And in him you too are being built together to become a dwelling in which God lives by his Spirit."

The point is this: we are each a block of stone that takes our place in building up God's house. We come from different places and backgrounds, no single story being the same as another, but the central focus of our story is that we come together to be a part of what God has planned. While we're being *placed* for God's purposes, God also *prepares* us for His purposes. Stepping into God's purposes for your life means you will often have to step out of what you have planned for yourself. The culture we live in places more emphasis on the position of our placement than our preparedness for placement. We'd rather be seen and out front, even if that means skipping a few steps in the hammering and chiseling process. If you want to be made into something quickly, if you want God to come into your life and work everything out in your timing, go ahead and skip a few steps and become a common piece of art. It can happen, but you will crumble because you weren't properly prepared.

Sharpening Our Ax

When I was a junior in high school, I took an English class, and the teacher had taken a particular interest in me. One afternoon I stayed after and had a conversation with her about an essay I'd been writing for her class. Ironically, I told her that one day I wanted to write a book, but I wasn't sure what it would be about. I had secretly developed a passion for words and eloquence, which wasn't necessarily the coolest thing to do in high school. She listened to me as I revealed these dreams to her, and then she told me this story about Abraham Lincoln.

I want to preface this by saying that she told me she wasn't sure whether this was true or not, but the point still stands. The rumor is that when Abraham Lincoln was just seven years old, he was already proficient with an ax. His family had to clear land for their farm, and he was put to work at a young age. Years later, when Lincoln was around seventeen, the locals were asking him to cut the wood for their fences. News of his wiry strength and abilities with an ax was traveling around the community. In Lincoln's presidential run, his skill with an ax was so well publicized that it essentially became a political symbol for him. It was a part of his campaign, but it didn't stop there—this is where she was less sure about the truth of the story, but the truth of the point remains.

During the Civil War, Lincoln visited the camp of some wounded soldiers, and one of them recalled watching good ol' Abe find an ax at the campsite. He picked it up and held it at arm's length for over a minute. Younger soldiers tried to copy him, but they couldn't get anywhere close to a minute. Supposedly, one of the soldiers asked President Lincoln, "Mr. President, what would you do if you had six hours to chop down a tree?" Lincoln responded, "I would spend the first four sharpening my ax."

God's purpose for your life may very well be that you will cut down trees, but the first four hours of the process require sharpening your ax. Everyone wants to celebrate the triumph and the spotlight that comes when we make that final swing that brings the tree down. But no one is there when you are sharpening your ax, in the quiet of the forest alone, just you and God. Those are the moments we all need to hear about but are rarely shared—the moments others couldn't see, the ones we didn't celebrate, the ones that made us into who we are, the ones that turned us from lumberwack to lumberjack.

The depth of your character must be great enough to anchor the height of your platform. Lincoln had perfected the ability to wield an ax from the time he was just a boy on his parent's property, cutting wood for his family and neighbors. Perhaps all those years chopping wood simply led him to become a great lumberjack, or perhaps God used it for more. A consistency and a diligence comes with chopping wood. Lincoln would certainly need those qualities during his presidency.

You might be wondering what it means to sharpen your ax, and you might be wondering why you're still in the position you're in—at that job, without that person, having to do the same things you've always done. We tend to misread where we're at because we're busy dreaming about where we want to be. What we fail to realize is that we can't be where we dream of being without being molded where we currently are. These are the four hours we need to spend sharpening our ax. Don't get discouraged if you're still cutting wood for your neighbors. You never know, it might help you when you're the president one day.

People want the spotlight, so they chase influence, but influence without character is corrosive. Those four hours in the forest, those moments in the quarry, that's where God forms the character within you that allows you to stay true to form and carry out the purposes God has called you to. You may have all the talent in the world—the strength to strike hard or the strength to hold much—but if you lack character, your talent will be compromised. You'll lose form, and your strength will be misguided. A part of your stone will be uneven, and the whole thing will crumble. These moments are precious. They're private, but they're purposeful.

God's Glory Is in Your Story

In John 9 we see one of Jesus's strangest miracles. It's not only strange but also kind of disgusting. There is a man who has been blind since birth, and Jesus heals him by spitting on the ground, making a muddy, clay-like substance, putting it on the man's eyes, and telling him to go and wash. There was a lot of brokenness in this man's life. He had physical limitations, and because of those physical limitations, we can be sure he had experienced some emotional battles and scars. But after his path intersects with Jesus, Jesus spits on the ground and makes a new creation that heals this man, not only from his physical blindness but from his spiritual blindness as well. It's through the sharing of this man's story that others around him become aware of God's glory and power of His Son, Jesus.

The miracle is strange, but it isn't random. Jesus is re-creating sight using the original method of creation. Man was first made by the dust of the ground, and through the dirt of the earth and

Jesus's saliva, this man is given his sight. He is alive and made new. If you think about it, this miracle was creative. After Jesus makes the mud and puts it on the man's eyes, He tells him to "go . . . wash in the Pool of Siloam" (John 9:7). The miracle isn't complete when Jesus puts the mud on the man's eyes; it requires the man to act in faith and go and wash. Jesus sends the man to a pool to wash, the Pool of Siloam. The Hebrew meaning of the English word "siloam" is "to send." This man who was born blind was sent to wash at a place that means sent, by Jesus, who was sent by God so that, "those who do not see may see" (John 9:39 ESV).

After this man receives his sight, people around him are in awe. They want to know how he can see. They've only ever known him as a blind beggar. They ask in verse 10, "How then were your eyes opened?" He responds, "The man they call Jesus made some mud and put it on my eyes. He told me to go to Siloam and wash. So I went and washed, and then I could see" (v. 11).

When the Pharisees hear this, they don't believe him. They try to get him to change his story, asking him over and over how his eyes were opened, and he says, "I have told you already and you did not listen. Why do you want to hear it again?" (v. 27). Finally, he says, "Nobody has ever heard of opening the eyes of a man born blind. If this man [Jesus] were not from God, he could do nothing" (vv. 32–33).

This man's story was messy, particularly for that day and time. People believed that the man was born blind because of sin, but Jesus said in John 9:3, "Neither this man nor his parents sinned . . . but this happened so that the works of God might be displayed in him." There were many physical, emotional, and social discomforts that created the messiness in his life, but after he receives his sight, he can't help but tell everyone about the grace, power, and glory of God. As hard as it may be to share our stories, especially those messy parts we would prefer to remain private, we have to remember that our stories aren't about us but about Jesus working in and through us. Like the story of the man born blind, God's glory shines brightest through the messiness of our stories.

We usually fall into one of two camps when we're faced with the opportunity to share our stories. For some of us, I think we're hesitant to share because we know how bad it is. We think it's *too* messy. We're ashamed of certain parts in our stories. We don't want to share the parts about where we were, what we did, whom we hurt, or who hurt us. We'll tell our stories, just not the shady parts. We don't want to make anyone feel uncomfortable or make them cringe, especially during those parts where they might feel bad for us. Honestly, though, what kind of story is that?

We all have times when it feels as though God isn't coming through, when it feels as if the enemy sent a blitz and God didn't call the right protection. I know God's promises are true, and I know that He hasn't left, that He is teaching, growing, stretching, and molding me, because every great story has chapters of trials. *Spoiler Alert*: what kind of story is *Star Wars* if Luke leaves out the part about Darth Vader being his dad? What kind of story is Cinderella if she doesn't have a wicked stepmother and a limited amount of time? *The Lord of the Rings* isn't a great story because of what Frodo was able to avoid but because of the things he accomplished despite the opposition and conflict. *Harry Potter* isn't a great story because he's an amazing wizard;

it's an amazing story because of what he overcomes with his friends and through the power of love. Don't be afraid to tell those messy parts of your story. Never be ashamed of what God has done for you, because what God has done for you, He can do for anybody. And nothing can overcome the cross. The cross is the binding of the book that holds our pages together, even the painful ones. Don't discount what God is setting you up for by revealing His glory through your story. The messiness of your story is what makes it relatable. Those are the chapters you can't put down. Your story isn't over. It was a bad page, a rough chapter, but God isn't done with it yet. He is still writing. Being a follower of Jesus doesn't mean we present ourselves as perfect in front of others. We need to share the story of healing behind the scars.

The other camp we fall into is the camp of thinking that our story isn't messy enough to be interesting. Even if your story doesn't have some crazy climax, according to the Bible, you were dead in your sin before you came to Jesus. You may not have been selling crystal meth to people in rehab or experimenting with black tar heroin in your free time, but according to Ephesians 2:5, it wasn't until you met Jesus that you truly came alive. In John 9 the people are essentially asking the man, Aren't you that blind filth that used to beg over there? And he says, I used to be that guy, but then I ran into Jesus. Isn't that our story as well? I was _____, but then I met Jesus. He wasn't afraid to share about the messiness, period.

When you felt like you were being cast out, when nobody else came looking for you, bruised and beaten up from your old ways, dead in your sin, blind, Jesus showed up. The glory of God in your story is that because of Jesus, you once were lost, but now you're found. You once were broken, but now you are restored. You once were blind, but now you see. You once were dead, but now you're alive. You cannot measure what God is doing with you and through you by the emotions of the moment. A few hours before coming into contact with Jesus, the blind man had no idea what God was about to do. He could have been the lowest he had ever been on that day, *but God.* He is doing immeasurably more than you could ask or imagine. He is working in you.

Work in and out of Me

In Philippians, Paul is under house arrest, which is a less than ideal circumstance to find yourself in, but Paul tells us in the first chapter that he is being imprisoned for Christ because he is advancing the gospel among the imperial guard, reflecting the light of Jesus even in his dark circumstances.

I love what he says in Philippians 2:12–13, "Therefore, my dear friends, as you have always obeyed—not only in my presence, but now much more in my absence—continue to work out your salvation with fear and trembling, for it is God who works in you to will and to act in order to fulfill his good purpose."

We have to work out what God works in! God works His will into us so that we can work out His will for us and the others around us. It pleases Him to do that, and it all starts in the shadows of the quarry. Away from the noise and distractions, God grabs His hammer and chisel and goes to work in us so that we are prepared to be placed for His purposes as we work out His will for us.

I don't think we look at the hammering and chiseling

process properly. It's always presented to us as a process where a lot of things wrong in us need to be hammered and chiseled away. We have to chisel away our pride, hammer out our anger. That's not wrong. But I think it is equally true and important for us to realize that the hammering and chiseling process is as much about God working His will into us so that we reflect His image as it is about chiseling undesirable things away. When Michelangelo saw that block of marble in the courtyard, he didn't just look at the parts that needed to be chiseled away; he looked at that block of marble and wanted to reveal everything it was meant to be. One of the great artists in history then slowly, carefully, and methodically worked his will into the marble, into what he knew it would become.

At one point, we each were an unwanted block, a messy inconvenience before we became the masterpiece of the King. That's when God, the Greatest Artist of All Time, came to us, got a hold of us, and went to work in our lives. A *David* can be made out of you. You're the exact kind of marble that Jesus came for—one riddled with imperfections and blemishes, one that others didn't think could be made into anything, one that didn't have an identity as it sat in the shadows for years. Your story becomes a testament to God's glory when it's surrendered into the hands of the Sculptor. Jesus came for the blocks that had been left behind, not the ones that graded out at the highest quality.

Jesus didn't come to make nearly perfect people into completely perfect people. He came while we were lost within our own messes, the victims of our own inability to navigate our way to God. We were sheep without a shepherd, and God sent His Son, Jesus, to infiltrate our messes and rescue us. Jesus said in Luke 19:10, "The Son of Man came to seek and to save the lost." While you stumbled in your blindness, unable to find Him, He found you. You were once a mess, but now you are being made into His masterpiece.

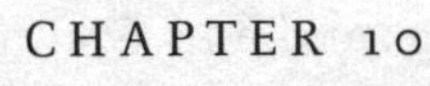

CHAPTER 10

The Art of Remembering

I suffer from spiritual amnesia. You probably do too.

God frequently calls His people to remember, not because He is a needy egomaniac but because we suffer from severe short-term memory loss. He doesn't need us to remember Him because He's insecure that we might forget, but because in our ignorance we tend to forget and then complain about the goodness of God to God.

Few things will test your patience like reading the book of Exodus. It's infuriating. In chapter 14, God miraculously splits the sea to provide safe passage for the Israelites, while striking down their enemies. In chapter 15, the Israelites are already complaining to Moses about how they have no water. In chapter 16, they begin to complain about how they have no food. Then in chapter 17, it's back to complaining about a lack of water. We're not even one chapter removed from one of the most miraculous displays of God's power and provision before the people begin to grumble. This vicious cycle continues, and you wish you could just grab a megaphone and ask these people, "Are you really complaining right now? Have you already forgotten the plagues and how God freed you from the bondage of the Egyptians? Has what transpired at the Red Sea already slipped your mind?" But it doesn't take long before we examine our own lives and conclude that we're no less frustrating than the Israelites. God calls us to remember in faith rather than react in doubt.

In Joshua 3 God performs a miracle similar to what happened at the Red Sea. As Joshua and the Israelites are preparing to cross the Jordan River and into the Promised Land, God stops the flow of the Jordan, allowing the Israelites to pass over on dry ground. What catches my attention is what happens afterward, in Joshua 4. God commands Joshua to take twelve men, each from a tribe of Israel, and have them pick up a stone from the Jordan River. God tells them in Joshua 4:6–7 that they need to take the stones and set them up "to serve as a sign among you. In the future, when your children ask you, 'What do these stones mean?' tell them that the flow of the Jordan was cut off. . . . These stones are to be a memorial to the people of Israel forever." No matter how messy our lives are or how mightily He delivers us from those messes, He knows a reminder would be helpful.

One Small Step for Man

On July 20, 1969, the lunar module, *Eagle,* detached from Apollo 11. Neil Armstrong and Buzz Aldrin were rocketing toward the moon, on their way to becoming the first humans to ever set foot on the lunar surface. As they touched down, Armstrong, the commander of the mission, uttered one of his famous quotes, as he announced to the world, "The *Eagle* has landed," and as he climbed down the ladder and stepped onto the moon's surface, he proclaimed, "That's one small step for a man, one giant leap for mankind." (Some of you are thinking I misquoted him here, but it's true. Armstrong said, "That's one small step for *a* man," not, "That's one small step for man."[1] Sorry for ruining your day.) While Aldrin roamed the moon's territory, he described it as "a magnificent desolation." They explored for two and a half hours as they collected samples and photographs. They set a plaque that said, "Here men from the planet Earth first set foot upon the moon. July 1969 A.D. We came in peace for all mankind," and planted the American flag before heading home.

I read an article about this trip to the moon that featured a photograph of Buzz Aldrin standing next to the American flag on the moon. Below the picture it said, "A space-clad Apollo astronaut stands proudly next to a red-white-and-blue American flag, his national trophy telling the lonely world 'the United States was here.'"[2]

If you and I were to step onto the moon, the first thing we might think is that it is a magnificent desolation, but then we'd be able to point to the flag and say, "The United States was here," and we would remember what took place decades before in the summer of '69. Armstrong's quote "That's one small step for a man, one giant leap for mankind" is so powerful because it's the recognition that in a moment as significant as being the first individual to ever set foot on the moon, Armstrong knew it wasn't a time to gloat about how incredible he was. It was a time to celebrate how far mankind had come. In the face of significant challenges in this world, when we see that American flag on the moon, even in photographs, we remember how even in the face of the impossible, there is hope that we can achieve the impossible. God tells Joshua to make a memorial. Why? So that when the Israelites looked back on it after undoubtedly forgetting how God was with them, they would remember the faithfulness of God, who was not only with them but for them.

The Call

Jesus had twelve disciples, but we don't know them all equally well. He had a smaller circle of three within his already small circle of twelve. James, John, and Peter get significantly more airtime than others, like Andrew or Bartholomew. But of them all, I'm not sure any stories stick with us quite like the stories of Peter.

For better or worse, I see a lot of myself in Peter. I think we all find bits of ourselves within his story as we read the gospels. He is impulsive. His thought process is: just do it, just say it. He lives life at a rapid pace, and he's kind of a hothead, perhaps has a bit of a hair-trigger personality, and because of his impulsiveness and ask-for-forgiveness-not-permission approach to life, the stories about him are wildly entertaining. Peter is the guy who gets out of the boat to walk on water toward Jesus in faith but also falls for lack of faith. When Jesus asks the disciples, "Who do people say I am?", all the other disciples look around at one another and are like, "Uhhh . . . John the Baptist? Elijah? A prophet like Jeremiah?" Then Jesus asks, "Who do you say that I am?" Peter doesn't hesitate: "You are the Messiah, the Son of the living God" (Matthew 16:16). Peter's highs are really high, and his lows are really low. Do you remember how Jesus calls Peter to follow Him?

In Luke 5:4–6, Jesus has just finished teaching a crowd of people from Simon's (Peter's) boat. After finishing His sermon, He turns to Peter and says, "'Put out into deep water and let down your nets for a catch.' 'Master,' Simon replied, 'we've worked hard all night long and caught nothing. But if you say so, I'll let down the nets.' When they did this, they caught a great number of fish, and their nets began to tear" (CSB).

Peter is really, really embarrassed. As a professional fisherman, the last thing he wants to admit is that he was unable to catch anything all night, and it certainly doesn't help that the carpenter is trying to tell the fisherman how to fish. I'm sure he's thinking, "Hey, man, I appreciate You wanting to help and everything, but I do this for a living, so, I'll give it one more shot just to humor You, but I'm not over here telling You how to make farmhouse tables." Reluctantly he obeys Jesus at His word and is astounded at the results. He falls at Jesus's feet and says in verse 8, "Go away from me, because I'm a sinful man, Lord," but Jesus says in verse 10, "Don't be afraid from now on you will be catching people" (CSB).

So much happens between this moment in Luke 5, when Jesus calls Peter to follow Him, and the night that Jesus is betrayed, but fast-forward with me to the night Jesus is betrayed. As the torches of the soldiers and Pharisees draw nearer and Judas betrays Jesus with a kiss, Peter comes running. As they arrest Jesus, Malchus, the high priest's servant, becomes the victim of Peter's impulsiveness. Peter draws his sword and cuts off Malchus's right ear before Jesus scolds him. Then they take Jesus away, and Peter follows at a distance.

He follows Jesus all the way to the courtyard of where He is being tried. Three times people ask Peter whether he knows Jesus or imply that he is a disciple of Jesus, and each time he denies even knowing Him. Jesus had predicted that before the rooster crowed Peter would deny Him three times. After the third denial, Matthew 26:74–75 says, "Immediately a rooster crowed. Then Peter remembered the word Jesus had spoken: 'Before the rooster crows, you will disown me three times.' And he went outside and wept bitterly."

That's the last we hear from Peter for a while. We're told that he went out weeping bitterly, but where? We don't see him. It isn't until the resurrection that he steps back onto the scene. When Jesus told Peter that he would deny Him three times, Peter basically said, "No way. I'd die for you. I won't deny you." The mess Peter is in makes ours seem miniscule, but Jesus wasn't done writing his story. He was about to call Peter to remembrance and restoration.

EpiPen Panic

When I was a kid, I had bad allergies. I mean really bad. It's one thing to sound nasally because you have allergies, but toss a little puberty in there, with your voice cracking every other word, and now you sound like a broken instrument. It was a nightmare, so I had to start taking allergy shots.

When we got to the clinic, they took me to the back, where they had me take off my shirt and made me lie on my stomach. I could feel the doctor start to prick my back multiple times. He said, "I'm injecting you with different substances to find out exactly what you're allergic to. This is going to make you itch, but it will help us in the long run." It was a burning itch. Needless to say, I wasn't excited about going back for shots multiple times a week. Mostly, though, I never had any issues. Except for this one time. It wasn't funny at the time, but now it's hilarious, so don't feel bad about laughing.

When my mom and I got home from the clinic one day, something didn't feel right. My throat felt swollen in a way I'd never felt before, and my skin had hives that were growing and multiplying. I looked in the mirror, and my eyes and face had started to swell. I looked like Will Smith in *Hitch*. I went downstairs to show my mom the hives, and it felt as though my throat was closing up more and more. I showed her and told her what was going on. She said, "I'm getting the EpiPen. You're having an allergic reaction."

For those of you who aren't well versed in allergic reactions, an EpiPen is an emergency shot that can be administered at home. Anaphylaxis, which is a fancy word for a severe allergic reaction, can kill you if you don't have an emergency dose of epinephrine lying around, which is where the EpiPen comes in. Epinephrine reverses anaphylaxis. For example, when I had this allergic reaction, my blood pressure started to drop as my blood vessels started to relax, and then my airway became constricted. Epinephrine constricts the blood vessels to raise blood pressure and relaxes the muscles in the airway to help with breathing.

Mom came running back into the kitchen with the EpiPen. At this point, I was freaking out. I knew this kind of reaction could kill you, but I was also pretty concerned about how painful this shot was going to be. We were both screaming at each other. Mom pulled up the sleeve of my shirt. (Yes, the EpiPen is normally administered in your thigh, but we were both panicking.) "Hold still!"

"Woah! What? You're just going to shoot me with this thing?!" I was panicking.

"That's how it works. Now be quiet and hold still!"

"You aren't the one who is dying and about to get shot!"

I felt her thrust the pen on my arm, but I was amazed at how painless it was. I didn't even feel a pinprick.

Mom screamed, "Ouch! Gosh, no! Owww!"

"What? What is it?"

"I accidentally shot me and not you! I shot myself in the thumb."

The needle had shot straight into her thumb because she held it upside down. Of course I didn't feel anything; I didn't get shot. We had to drive to the clinic and get a new shot. Thankfully I lived. Meanwhile, Mom's thumb looked like it might fall off, so she had to go to the emergency room. The entire evening was chaotic.

As I sat in the office with my doctor, waiting to make sure my reaction was calming down, I got an education on how allergy shots work. I asked him, "I thought allergy shots were supposed to stop reactions? Why did I have an allergic reaction after getting allergy shots?"

He said, "Luke, the way allergy shots work is that we inject you with a small amount of the very allergens that you're allergic to. We try to make sure we give you just enough to stimulate your immune system but not too much that you have a reaction like you had tonight. Sometimes this happens, but the way it works is that over time we introduce what you're allergic to into your system so that your system builds up a tolerance to the allergen, and that will stop your allergies from being so severe."

"So . . . you shot me with the thing that could have killed me?"

"That's one way to look at it. But we give you just enough to make your system stronger. That's the amazing thing about allergy shots. What could technically end your life brings an allergy-free life. Every time you get allergy shots, your body gets better at remembering the allergen and learns how to react."

Our relationship with God is a lot like our body's relationship with allergy shots. Our body remembers the allergens it has received in the past, so it knows how to react in the moment. The more we reflect on what God has done for us in the past, the more likely we will react in faith in the middle of the messiness of life. It's important to pause, rest, and remember the faithfulness of God in what He has provided and withheld. The more we remember, the better we react. Sometimes God has to help us remember, and Jesus certainly helps Peter remember in John 21.

The Call Back

In John 21 Jesus has already been tried, crucified, and raised. Peter and six other disciples decide to go fishing, but despite fishing on the Sea of Galilee all night, they end up catching nothing. But come morning, something interesting happens.

> When daybreak came, Jesus stood on the shore, but the disciples did not know it was Jesus. "Friends," Jesus called to them, "you don't have any fish, do you?"
>
> "No," they answered.
>
> "Cast the net on the right side of the boat," he told them,

> "and you'll find some." So they did, and they were unable to haul it in because of the large number of fish. The disciple, the one Jesus loved, said to Peter, "It is the Lord!"
>
> When Simon Peter heard that it was the Lord, he tied his outer clothing around him (for he had taken it off) and plunged into the sea. Since they were not far from land (about a hundred yards away), the other disciples came in the boat, dragging the net full of fish.
>
> John 21:4–8 CSB

Do you remember how Jesus first called Peter to follow Him? They went fishing together. Do you remember the circumstances of that fishing trip? The night before, Peter had caught nothing. The next morning Jesus told him to cast his net again. Peter did as Jesus said, and when they tried to haul the net back up, it was so full of fish that it almost broke the net. Peter is in a much different place now than he was then. He has followed Jesus for years, walked with Him, eaten with Him, drank with Him, and done life with Him, but he has also denied Him. Did you catch the similarities between when Jesus calls Peter to follow Him and what happens in John 21? It's the same miracle. The night before, the disciples caught nothing. The next morning Jesus tells them to cast their net again. When they follow His instructions, the net becomes so full that they can't haul it in. The Scripture tells us that when Jesus was on the shore, the disciples didn't realize it was Him.

John is the one who screams, "It is the Lord!" But I believe Peter started to add things up before John ever said anything. Peter was the one who plunged into the water to race to the shore. He was eager to see Jesus, but there had to be some shame, uneasiness, and possibly fear that Jesus would be upset with him. He had seen Jesus since the resurrection, but who knows whether they had discussed what happened? Had they talked about the three denials? It didn't matter. Peter couldn't help himself; he had seen this miracle before.

When Jesus first calls Peter, Jesus tells him to cast his net, and it fills with fish. After Peter denies Jesus, He shouts to Peter from the shore to cast his net, and it fills with fish. When we find ourselves in a mess, God calls us to remember His faithfulness, not our failures. The same miracle Jesus performed to call Peter to first follow Him was the same miracle He performed to urge Peter to remember Him. Peter remembered, and he ran toward Jesus, not away from Him. There is something for us to learn in that. So often we feel as though our sin and the messiness of our lives puts us in a position where we need to get our lives together before coming back to God, before coming to Him in prayer or opening up His Word, but no. That's backward. In the messiest moments of life, take the plunge and storm the shores of grace. Your Savior isn't waiting to chastise you. He's making breakfast for you on the shore, inviting you to sit at His table. You don't have to be clean to come to Jesus. When you come to Jesus, He makes you clean. Peter was in a mess—he had failed, he denied Jesus three times—but that wasn't where his story ended, and it's not where your story ends.

In my own experience, the deepest disappointment we experience as sinful people is not the disappointment we feel when someone has let us down but the disappointment we feel when we have let someone else down. I would much rather be the one who receives disappointment than the one who delivers it. Peter's greatest disappointment had to be the denial of Jesus—he let Him down. Even though Jesus knew it was going to happen, that probably didn't make Peter feel any better.

After eating breakfast Jesus and Peter shared a life-changing conversation:

> Jesus asked Simon Peter, "Simon, son of John, do you love me more than these?"
>
> "Yes, Lord," he said to him, "you know that I love you."
>
> "Feed my lambs," he told him. A second time he asked him, "Simon, son of John, do you love me?"
>
> "Yes, Lord," he said to him, "you know that I love you."
>
> "Shepherd my sheep," he told him.
>
> He asked him the third time, "Simon, son of John, do you love me?"
>
> Peter was grieved that he asked him the third time, "Do you love me?" He said, "Lord, you know everything; you know that I love you."
>
> "Feed my sheep."
>
> John 21:15–17 CSB

Three times Peter denies Jesus; three times Jesus asks Peter whether he loves Him; three times Jesus gives Peter the command to carry out the work that still needed to be done. A lot of us look at our own version of denying Jesus—those messes in our own lives, those moments when we feel as if we've let God down or been a disappointment to Him—and we think that's it. We don't see the opportunity to be restored and recommissioned to continue to do the work God called us to. If Jesus extended grace to Peter after being denied three times, He isn't going to withhold grace from you.

Notice what Jesus *doesn't* ask. He doesn't ask, "Peter, will you promise to never fail Me again? Peter, will you be perfect from now on? Peter, will you apologize to the rest of us here? It really hurt My feelings when you denied Me, man. That was rude and mean. None of these other guys denied Me, but here you are eating My fish. You can't sit with us!"

What Jesus does ask is, "Simon, son of John, do you love me?" Above all else, Jesus wants your heart. Followers of Jesus won't always follow Him perfectly, but if we love Him, that is enough. He can work with whatever mess is in your life, but He needs your heart.

I read a commentary on this passage suggesting that Jesus addressed Peter as Simon, son of John, because Peter means "rock." When Peter denied Jesus, he lost the right to be called "rock" because he had failed to be the rock of faithfulness the night Jesus was arrested. While that makes some sense, I don't think it falls in line with the character of Jesus. I don't think Jesus would use this opportunity to shame Peter any more than he has already shamed himself. The hardest person to forgive is often ourselves. When Jesus asked a third time whether Peter loved Him, the Bible says that Peter was grieved. He knew that Jesus had just asked the question for a third time and that was the same number of times he had denied Jesus. I think Jesus addressed him as Simon, son of John, because that was Peter's birth name. He addressed him with his birth name as a way of signaling a fresh start. Jesus is telling Peter that his identity is in Him, not what he has done. He is reminding Peter of who He is.

Remember Jesus

I was eleven when my parents first found out that I had looked at pornography on our family computer. Ironically, that was also the first time I had ever looked at pornography. I didn't even try to cover my tracks, because I didn't know what I was getting into. I'm sure they simply saw the computer's history and caught me red-handed. I had heard about it at school and looked it up when I got home. I knew it was wrong, but I didn't realize how devastating it was and would become in this generation. It ruins marriages, distorts God's intention for sex between a husband and wife, and objectifies women.

I remember my dad walking upstairs, and I just knew something was off. His shoulders were slumped, and he walked slowly, like he had to break bad news. He confronted me about it, and I lied. I lied straight to his face, but it was a childlike lie, you know? The one that is literally not possible, but you swear by it anyway. Our computer was old, and I suggested to him that there was a glitch in the computer or something. If you were grading lies, that was an *F*.

Finally, we got to a point where I had to admit it. I cried. I felt terrible. I could tell I had let my dad down, and I knew I had done something wrong. But I remember him saying, "Luke, we know that you will mess up sometimes, but no matter what you do, we will always love you. This is something to learn from, not something to feel ashamed of. I'm glad I caught you, because now you know how dangerous it is and we can move forward."

The messes in your life may seem insurmountable, but from the shores of grace, Jesus is calling out to you to cast your net again and to remember His goodness. Where Peter thought there was completion, Jesus extended grace and gave him a continuation. It wasn't Peter's performance but his proclamation that Jesus is the Son of God, that he loved Him, and that he would follow Him that determined whether he could be used by God. Peter denied Jesus three times but went on to be one of the key leaders in the church. Your greatest failures don't kill your calling; faithlessness does. You don't have to run from God. Rather, take the plunge and run toward Him. Remember who He is and what He has done. Remember the calling He has proclaimed over your life. Remember Jesus's words to Peter: "Follow me." Those are His words to you too.

CHAPTER 11

By the Blood

I have a secret fear and insecurity: that I won't be accepted.

I've struggled with this since I was a kid. I vividly remember walking through the hallways of McKamy Middle School. Kids had braces, pimples, and all the other glorious perks of being thirteen. That was what you could see on the outside, but only I was keenly aware of how messy things were in my mind. I was highly concerned about appearing to be *enough* in the eyes of my peers. Was I athletic enough? Funny enough? Known enough? You might read that and think that's ridiculous, that was in middle school! But do we not do this still? I know I do.

Even as I write this, I have to fight the fear that my writing won't be accepted. I have to fight the insecurity of feeling like I'm not called to do what I do. I have to fight the insecurity of feeling as if I may never break through the barriers that are currently holding me back from harvesting the dreams God has planted in my heart.

Don't we all fear that we may not be accepted? Do we not wonder whether we are funny, smart, attractive, stylish, or talented enough? Few things sting like the pain of feeling as though you don't measure up, you're not good enough, your mess is *too* messy, and that a gap of separation the size of the Grand Canyon falls between where you are and where you wish you could be. We all pray that we will be able to break through beyond the confines of the mess we're in and fearlessly walk into the destiny God has prepared for us.

I grew up in the church. I sang the songs about the blood of Jesus and heard the messages about it, but I always wondered, How does the blood of Jesus give me power? The blood of Jesus covers our sins (Hebrews 9:22). The blood of Jesus is our redemption (1 Peter 1:18–19). Because of His blood, we have been clothed in His righteousness (2 Corinthians 5:21; 1 Peter 2:24). But is that it? I know those things are more than enough and completely undeserved, and even at that time, I knew it meant a lot, but it didn't necessarily make sense how we had power by the blood of Christ. Maybe I had been accepted by God, but where was the breakthrough? I still struggled, I still stumbled, and I still had messes in my life and battles that I faced. There was a veil over my thinking. I just had to walk through it.

Separation Anxiety

In biblical times the temple was of central importance to the Jewish people. The temple had two sections. The first section was called the Holy Place and the second was the innermost part of the temple called the Most Holy Place.

In Herod's temple a massive, intricately woven veil separated these two sections. It was essentially a curtain unlike any other: sixty feet high, thirty feet wide, and about four inches thick. It was woven together by beautiful blue, purple, and scarlet yarns and linens. But despite its size and beauty, the curtain was a constant reminder that sin separated humanity from God.

Only one person on one day each year could enter the innermost part of the temple. The high priest could enter the Most Holy Place on the Day of Atonement. He would carry out intricate rituals to atone for the sins of the people, and one of those rituals was sprinkling the blood of goats and bulls to appease the wrath of God for the sins of the people.

In my own life, I felt as though I was on the wrong side of the curtain. Accepted enough to stand in that first section but not quite to the point where I could break through beyond the curtain that separated me from truly knowing Christ and the power of His blood. I wanted to know Him deeper and more intimately, but I couldn't begin a deeper relationship with Him until I understood that I didn't need to wait until the messiness of my life was cleaned up. I could come to Him with the messiness of my life.

A few years ago, I was flying from L.A. to Atlanta, and my anxiety increased exponentially when I heard over the intercom: "We will begin the boarding process shortly." I don't know whether you have ever experienced this before, but let me just say this—the boarding process is either a source of great pride or great shame, depending on your status with the airline. Some people basically live on planes, and then some fly on an occasional holiday, and you can tell who they are.

The gate agent came over the intercom and started announcing who could board. "We are now boarding all active military members, those who need assistance, and those with children under the age of two." All right, those make sense. I could get down with this first group. But then the ranking continued.

"All Platinum and Platinum Medallion members may now feel free to board." Whatever. I didn't even know what those meant, so I assumed I definitely didn't fall into that category. "Now boarding all Gold and Gold Medallion members."

At this point I'm thinking, "Is this for real? Can we just get to Zone 4 over here! They are calling all members of the periodic table of elements!" It feels like they're picking on you. It's like they call you out by not calling you at all.

And then finally, "Now accepting the one gentleman remaining who will be duct-taped to the wing."

Maybe you've never felt excluded and separated from everyone else by an airline, but I'd be willing to bet that we've all had moments when we feel as if we've been excluded and separated from God. Maybe you feel like you're seen as enough in the eyes of God to get on the plane, but not quite enough to board with other people who are crushing this whole Christianity thing. Everyone else gets called to board, and you helplessly wait, hoping they let you on. You're praying for breakthrough.

Welcome to Breakthrough

As Jesus hung on the cross, immediately after He cried out, "It is finished," Matthew 27:51 says, "the curtain of the temple was torn in two from top to bottom."

The Bible says it was torn in two, *from top to bottom.*

Completely torn. Jesus had paid the price, and it was more than sufficient. Knowing how large the curtain was, it makes it easier to understand that this was a powerful, dramatic, miraculous representation of how Jesus's sacrifice on the cross was a once-and-for-all atonement for sin, for all people, for all time. Jesus had said, "I am the way, and the truth, and the life. No one comes to the Father except through me" (John 14:6). The tearing of the curtain was proof of what Jesus had already proclaimed.

"Therefore, brothers and sisters, since we have confidence to enter the Most Holy Place by the blood of Jesus, by a new and living way opened for us through the curtain, that is, his body" (Hebrews 10:19–20).

At the Last Supper, Jesus broke the bread and said, "This is my body given for you" (Luke 22:19). Then He poured the wine into the cup and said, "This cup is the new covenant in my blood, which is poured out for you" (v. 20).

The way to the Father is through Him. Jesus's body was the curtain that was torn. There was a new way, a new covenant that was established through Jesus's suffering. His body was torn, and His blood was spilled. The curtain was torn, and His blood had been sprinkled. Perfect atonement. Even the colors of the material that the curtain was made of indicated the condition of Christ's body—blue, purple, and scarlet. Jesus's flesh was blue and purple from the beating, and His blood ran scarlet red as He was flogged and crucified.

Where is the power in the blood of Jesus? Where is the breakthrough? Here in Ephesians 2:13–18:

> But now in Christ Jesus you who once were far away have been brought near by the blood of Christ.

> For he himself is our peace, who has made the two groups one and has destroyed the barrier, the dividing wall of hostility, by setting aside in his flesh the law with its commands and regulations. His purpose was to create in himself one new humanity out of the two, thus making peace, and in one body to reconcile both of them to God through the cross, by which he put to death their hostility. He came and preached peace to you who were far away and peace to those who were near. For through him we both have access to the Father by one Spirit.

The breakthrough is this: that you who were once far off have been brought near by the blood of Jesus. His flesh was broken down and torn so that there is no longer separation between humanity and God, and you—yes, you—have access to the God of heaven. The God who spoke the world into existence, the God who formed the galaxies and creates something out of nothing listens to you when you speak to Him. He knows you, loves you, and He even *likes* you. You're not just some child who He has to love because the Bible says He needs to. God actually likes you, and it is His joy to be your Father.

Now some of you read that and think that applies to some of us but not to you. Your mess is the mother of all messes. But you have to remember who wrote these words. Paul wrote Ephesians. He wrote Ephesians 2:13–18, and he wrote Ephesians 3:12, which says that in Christ Jesus "we have *boldness* and *access* with *confidence* through our faith in him" (ESV, emphasis added). Paul had persecuted the Christian church, murdered followers of Jesus. He is proof that you can't even murder your way out of grace.

Did you notice that Ephesians 2:13 doesn't specify how far away you were? It just says that you've been brought near. You have never been so far off in your sins that the blood of Christ couldn't bring you near. You may feel as though your failures run too deep to be cleansed, but Jesus's blood has never seen a stain that couldn't be washed clean, and that didn't change starting with you. Hebrews 4:16 tells us we can confidently approach the throne of grace to find mercy and grace in our time of need. Grace doesn't condone your sin, but it doesn't condemn you either. There is no condemnation for those who are in Christ Jesus (Romans 8:1). You don't have to love God from a distance; you can fall asleep in the arms of your Father, knowing He loves you. God is faithful to carry out His promises, and one of those promises is that your mess won't separate you from the love of God. "Who shall separate us from the love of Christ? Shall trouble or hardship or persecution or famine or nakedness or danger or sword? . . . No, in all these things we are more than conquerors through him who loved us. For I am convinced that neither death nor life, neither angels nor demons, neither the present nor the future, nor any powers, neither height nor depth, nor anything else in all creation, will be able to separate us from the love of God that is in Christ Jesus our Lord" (Romans 8:35, 37–39).

Don't spend a single second of your day trying to convince yourself that your mess leaves you on the other side of the curtain. The curtain wasn't torn so that we could sit back and wonder whether our mess is too much to step through. It was torn so that we can enter God's presence with confidence. You've been made clean by the blood of Jesus. You're wasting your time if you're waiting to get your life in order before you come to God. You can come to Him now. Step through. There is no longer separation between you and God. Breakthrough is not near; it's here.

When Will It Change?

I told you that my secret fear and insecurity is that I won't be accepted. Allow me to explain the timeline of my own messiness.

When I was in middle school, there was a girl who was considered popular, whatever that means. The word on the street was that she was throwing a party, and if you got invited, that meant you were probably popular too. I barely knew this girl, but all I wanted was to be invited to this party so that I would be accepted. I wanted that to be my breakthrough into middle school popularity. Ridiculous, isn't it? I got invited, but nothing changed.

Basketball tryouts started later that fall. All I wanted was to be on the middle school A-team. I agonized over this. I worried myself sick that if I wasn't accepted on the A-team, I'd be seen as less than. In middle school, as long as you have decent coordination and are taller than five feet five, you have a good chance of making the team. I was about five feet nine and athletic, so naturally, I had a good shot. I felt as if that would be my breakthrough to being seen as successful in the eyes of my peers. Ridiculous, isn't it? I made the A-team, but nothing changed.

I got to high school. My family moved to Minneapolis from Dallas that summer. I was so upset. I had to start all over. I wanted to make the freshman A-team because I thought it would be my breakthrough to being accepted by new friends. I made the A-team and made a lot of friends, but before the season started, I made my new friends laugh by making fun of our coach's nasal Midwest accent. True story, I didn't know he was behind me. We didn't like each other after that, and he made me split my time between teams. We were verbally confrontational with one another, but I didn't care. Sure, I cared about basketball, but not as much as I cared about being liked. I was accepted because people thought I was funny and cool. I got invited to the parties and knew all the people. I thought this was my breakthrough. Ridiculous, isn't it? I successfully started all over, but nothing changed.

Going into my sophomore year of high school, my family moved back to Dallas. The same school system and everything. I started attending the high school I would have gone to after middle school had we never moved to Minneapolis. Nothing was the same. I had a lot of the same friends as I had before, but things were different. They knew different people. I was playing catch-up. I got back into basketball, but I felt so behind. I knew nothing about this high school and the way they did things. I thought that would be the breakthrough I needed to get back on track in life. Ridiculous, isn't it? I made the team, but nothing changed.

Now I missed Minneapolis. I missed my friends there and the normalcy I'd established. My parents flew me back to Minneapolis often, only because they felt bad that they had moved me so much during high school. While I was visiting friends in Minneapolis, I got a text from my mom that my dog wasn't doing well. Pause. We are dog people, dogs-are-family type people, weirdly obsessed-with-our-dog type people. I got back to Dallas, and he seemed to be better, but while I was eating lunch the following week, my advisor came and got me. My mom met me outside with big sunglasses on, sobbing because we had to go put my dog down. I hadn't really had much experience with death, and that messed me up. I had to go back into the high school and get assignments from the classes I would miss because I was busy watching my dog die.

I had tears streaming down my face, my eyes were puffy, and of course, as I walked into the school, the cheerleaders were all sitting in the hallway I had to walk through to get my missed assignments. I had gone to homecoming with one of them, and she saw that something was wrong. She asked me what had happened, hugged me for a while, and I just cried. I went to the basketball coach and quit the team. Eventually he asked me to come back, and I did, but then they cut everyone on our team that wasn't six feet five or taller, had super involved family members, or was likely to play in college. I thought that was extreme until I learned that his son and his son's team that he had been coaching for a decade were about to be in high school, and it made sense. I was really starting to get bitter about things in my life. I even told my mom that I didn't believe in the Bible or Jesus anymore. I was scattered. So I started drinking and smoking on the weekends, especially when I went back to Minnesota. I thought that would help me be accepted by a new crowd of friends and help me break through my bitterness. Ridiculous, isn't it? I kept drinking, but nothing changed.

By the end of my senior year, I started to become more self-aware of the power I had over my own life. I didn't know what I wanted to do with it, but I knew I wanted to do something. Even in the messiness of my desire to be accepted by anyone and everyone, I could feel God poking and prodding me to give Him my attention. I ended up following friends to college my freshman year, and they all decided they were going to join fraternities. I knew I would excel if I joined a fraternity, but that was the problem. I would excel in the wrong areas and activities. I decided not to "rush" with the rest of the freshman class, and to be honest, that freshman year was the loneliest year of my life. I needed that year of loneliness to find breakthrough and become who I am today. Sounds ridiculous, doesn't it? But I started pursuing Jesus, and everything changed.

I transferred to Texas A&M University and got involved with a great group of guys. I started going with them to Breakaway, a massive Bible study on the campus of Texas A&M. God stirred up passions in my heart that I didn't even understand. I started writing, got opportunities to preach, and met people that would be instrumental in helping me shape my faith. Don't be fooled, though. I'm not trying to make it sound as if I started following Jesus and a life of perfection began. That's not it at all. There were a lot of lessons learned and challenges to be faced, but I tell you all that to tell you this: one of the messes I've had to deal with my entire life is this insatiable desire to be accepted by others, but it wasn't until I started pursuing Jesus that I was able to satisfy that desire and find true breakthrough by His blood.

The Pressing and Passion of Jesus

My favorite moment in the gospels is one of the most unsettling moments in the gospels, but it shows us what Jesus went through to save us.

It's Thursday night. The disciples are having difficulty staying awake, despite Jesus insisting that they stay up and pray. The disciples hit snooze, but deep within the bowels of the garden of Gethsemane, Jesus knows His hour has come. What He is about to endure is so unfathomable that a word was created to describe the brutality and pain of His suffering. The word "excruciating" can be traced back to its Latin roots in the 1500s. It comes from the Latin word *excruciatus*, meaning "to crucify" or "to cause pain or anguish to." Jesus is fervently praying that the Father would take this cup from Him. He knows His betrayer is nearby with a band of guards and soldiers. Christ sweats drops of blood, agonizing in prayer, but He is prepared to step into the Father's plan. Our King was beginning the pressing process.

The word "Gethsemane" means "oil press." Traditionally, kings of Israel were anointed with oil, but there can be no oil unless you first press and crush the olive. Do you see the significance embedded in this scene? Our King was crushed for us so that His people could be anointed by His blood and be made clean.

In his masterful work *My Utmost for His Highest*, Oswald Chambers described that night in Gethsemane so beautifully. He says,

> We can never fully comprehend Christ's agony in the Garden of Gethsemane, but at least we don't have to misunderstand it. It is the agony of God and man in one Person, coming face to face with sin. We cannot learn about Gethsemane through personal experience. Gethsemane and Calvary represent something totally unique—they are the gateway into life for us. . . . The agony in Gethsemane was the agony of the Son of God in fulfilling His destiny as the Savior of the world. The curtain is pulled back here to reveal all that it cost

> Him to make it possible for us to become sons of God. His agony was the basis for the simplicity of our salvation. The Cross of Christ was a triumph for the *Son of Man*. It was not only a sign that our Lord had triumphed, but that He had triumphed to save the human race. Because of what the Son of Man went through, every human being has been provided with a way of access into the very presence of God.[1]

Unlimited Access, Unlimited Power

Because of this cosmic breakthrough, you have access into the very presence of God. Not *if* your mess gets cleaned up, but *because* His blood has cleaned your mess up. You don't walk into His presence as a stranger either, but as sons and daughters of the King. I want you to understand this: there is no sin too stubborn for the blood of Jesus. God's grace doesn't stop where your sin starts, and there has never been a mess in your life that the cross cowers at. So many of us are looking for fulfillment from other things that will take us into a more satisfactory place than the one we are currently in. We look to our marriage, grades, whom we're dating, salaries, appearances, or whatever it may be, but nothing can stand in the gap where Jesus hung. It is only by the blood of Jesus that we can confidently enter the presence of God, where every desire we could ever have is fulfilled and every dream we could ever have dreamed pales in comparison to the reality of who God is and what He has done by sending His Son to make a way for us. His blood gives us life. That is the power. This is the breakthrough you've been searching for.

CHAPTER 12

Bring the Broken Home

The epidemic sweeping our nation in the winter of 2013 was causing unparalleled pandemonium. It was during that winter that Disney released the movie *Frozen*, and life as we knew it would never be the same. Before I saw it in theatres, I knew the songs by heart because they were everywhere. For months I was asked, "Do you want to build a snowman?" or told to "Let it go! Let it go!"

Do you remember when Elsa's powers hit her sister, Anna, in the head? Anna is healed, but her memory has to be wiped, and the aftermath of the accident is worse than the accident itself. Elsa basically becomes a prisoner in her own home, locked in her room full of fear and shame because of the accident. She loses the bond she once had with her sister, and by the time Elsa is forced to come out of her room, it's supposed to be a day of celebration for her coronation. But she can't even enjoy it because the shame and fear run so deeply that she is constantly worried about what may go wrong.

Things get messy at the coronation after-party. In her anger, Elsa accidentally releases her powers in front of everybody. The look on her face is one of disbelief. Her worst fears have been realized. People have seen parts of her life that she didn't want anyone to know about, and in her embarrassment, fear, and shame, she runs away. She doesn't start an ice drug cartel or go off on a bender. She doesn't even become a terrible person or the evil character in the story.

Elsa runs deep into the woods, as far away as she can from friends and family, and she starts putting the walls back up she has always known. She makes a gigantic ice castle and goes back to living the life she was used to—a life of isolation, surrounded by walls built by shame and fear. She thinks she isn't fit to be a queen. She doesn't believe she is normal enough to be a part of her community. She wonders whether she could ever be loved like this, even by her own family. The problem is that she fails to understand the character of a family that loves her.

Have you ever met someone who has a tantalizing testimony? Something that sounds like it was straight out of a fiction novel? They start telling you their story and it's like, "Well, it was a dark and stormy night. I was drunk and stoned. I don't even know what country I was in. I stumbled out of the strip club and passed out in the alleyway behind it, and suddenly, it was then that I thought, 'Maybe I should give Jesus a try.' And now here I am, a missionary reaching the farthest corners of the earth to declare the good news of our Lord and Savior Jesus Christ." Maybe that's your story. If it is, that's amazing. But for most of us, our story is a lot like Elsa's. The story of our life and our relationship with God is that we don't feel like we're that bad, but we know that we're definitely not that good either. We're not living the worst life ever, but it's a life that is more isolated and separated from God than we care to admit. We have wounds, stories of shame and embarrassment, horrors we've experienced or instigated. We've created a mess of a life and it makes us feel as though we can't be a part of God's family, that we couldn't possibly be called a son or daughter of God, and certainly that we couldn't live under His roof in heaven, so we run.

That's when we are forgetting the character of our Father in heaven. These waves of worry and tsunamis of shame come beating down the shores of our hearts. Rather than seeing a loving Father, we wallow in our guilt and shame and ask ourselves, "What is wrong with me? How could God ever love someone like me?"

This Is What God Thinks of You

The more secure we are in what our Father thinks of us and the more certain we are of His character, the less likely we are to run from Him because of the messiness in our lives.

In Matthew 3 Jesus comes to the Jordan River to be baptized by His cousin and forerunner, John the Baptist. Jesus has yet to start His public ministry. He hasn't preached His most famous sermon, and He hasn't performed His most famous miracles. As John raises Jesus from the water, Matthew 3:16–17 (ESV) says, "And when Jesus was baptized, immediately he went up from the water, and behold, the heavens were opened to him, and he saw the Spirit of God descending like a dove and coming to rest on him; and behold, a voice from Heaven said, 'This is my beloved Son, with whom I am well pleased.'"

Did you catch that last bit?

Before Jesus has even done anything, God calls Him beloved. Do you want to know what God thinks of you? If you've repented of your sin and believe in Jesus as the Son of God, your sins—past, present, and future—have been forgiven. God is pleased with you in the same way He is pleased with Jesus. How is that possible? Because of what Jesus has done. It has nothing to do with what we have done, and that's good news. God's character is unshakable, and He unconditionally loves His people. The dastardliest messes in your life cannot destroy the love God feels for you.

Covenants are an important thread throughout the Bible, and the new covenant is one God has made between Him and us. God established the new covenant through Christ. In Matthew 5:17 Jesus says that He came to fulfill the law, and He did. What God thinks of you is covenantal, not conditional. You are justified by grace alone, through faith alone, on the foundation of Christ alone. What God thinks of you is not contingent on your own abilities; it is solidified through Christ's actions. The enemy will use the messes in your life to distract you from the blood of Jesus. He will try to use your failures to sabotage your faith. But God doesn't work around your failures. He works in them, through them, and frees you from them. God didn't work around the cross; He hung on it. Jesus willingly went to the cross, passionately endured the suffering that we deserved, and victoriously stepped out of the tomb over sin and death.

If you think your mess it too messy, if you think you've failed too often, if you think you've done or experienced things that are too shameful or horrific to come home to God, may I tell you something that may hurt a little bit but will ultimately help you heal? You don't have that kind of power. Your mess doesn't have that kind of power. To say that your mess is too much is to say that the cross is too little. The power of the cross is greater than the messiness of your life and the feelings you feel. You are not called to stay in that tomb. You can't outrun a love that knows no bounds.

ABC

In John 11 Jesus returned to Bethany to see His family friends, Lazarus, Mary, and Martha. Unfortunately, Lazarus had been sick for a while and died days earlier. His body had already been in the tomb for four days when Jesus and the disciples arrived. Jesus, the disciples, and the sisters of Lazarus went to the tomb where Lazarus's body was laid to rest. It was a cave with a stone placed across the entrance. Jesus said, "Take away the stone," and Martha chimed in, "Lord, by this time there will be an odor, for he has been dead four days" (v. 39 ESV). Jesus asked her, "Did I not tell you that if you believe, you will see the glory of God?" (v. 40). They removed the stone, and Jesus shouted into the tomb, "Lazarus, come out!" (v. 43). And at the sound of His voice, Lazarus was called back to life.

John 11 is one of my favorite passages of Scripture because it beautifully shows how we can come to God with our mess, particularly when we look at Martha. We are all Marthas. But three steps help bring our messes to God: approach God honestly, bank on God, and choose to see God's glory. I call these the ABCs. I haven't perfected them, but they have helped me immensely, and I'm believing they will help you too.

Approach God Honestly

After Lazarus had died and his sister Martha had heard Jesus was on His way to see them, she did something amazing. "When Martha heard that Jesus was coming, she went out to meet him" (John 11:20). Do you see that? Jesus was on His way to see her, but she *went and met* Him. Sometimes, in the messiness of our lives, we wait for God to come to us and give us clear instructions on what to do next. We want Him to approach us, but we can approach Him. God is already with you in your mess. You might as well approach Him and do it with honesty.

Look at what Martha says when she meets Jesus in John 11:21 (ESV), "Lord, if you had been here, my brother would not have died." I don't think this sounded the way we've heard it taught. Yes, it's a profession of faith in Jesus and His power, but I think Martha is frustrated with Jesus. Have you ever found yourself in a mess and felt like asking, "Jesus, where were You?" Martha is showing us that faith and frustration are not mutually exclusive. She approaches Him honestly, and so can we. Where were You, Jesus? Why are You being silent? Why is this happening to my child? Why is my marriage in shambles? Where are You in this illness? Honest, ugly prayers are specific prayers, and they bring more glory to God as He brings us deeper into His will and understanding of what He is doing and how He is working. Get ugly and approach Him honestly. God isn't afraid to go there with you; He's already there.

Bank on God

Martha was frustrated, but her faith was greater than her frustration. She knew she could bank on God to come through.

> "I know that even now God will give you whatever you ask."
>
> Jesus said to her, "Your brother will rise again."
>
> Martha answered, "I know he will rise again in the resurrection at the last day."
>
> Jesus said to her, "I am the resurrection and the life. The one who believes in me will live, even though they die; and whoever lives by believing in me will never die. Do you believe this?"
>
> "Yes, Lord," she replied, "I believe that you are the Messiah, the Son of God, who is to come into the world."
>
> John 11:22–27

Banking on God comes down to one thing: Do you believe that Jesus is who He says He is? Martha concedes that even though her brother has died, she believes that Jesus is able to work in the messiest of situations. Jesus asks us the same question He asked Martha, "Whoever believes in me shall never die. Do you believe this?"

God is working for our good and His glory, even in the mess. Do you believe it? That even death is not insurmountable? If you approach God honestly and believe that Jesus is who He says He is, then you can be certain that your mess matters to Him and that He can work a miracle in it. You can bank on God.

Choose to See God's Glory

When Jesus gets to the tomb where Lazarus is buried, He says, "Take away the stone." Martha is not down with that idea. "Lord, by this time there will be an odor, for he has been dead four days" (v. 39 ESV). Jesus responds in John 11:40, "Did I not tell you that if you believe, you will see the glory of God?"

We can approach God honestly and truly believe that we can bank on God to come through, even if it's not in the way we had anticipated or hoped for. But will we let Him into every area of our lives? So often we want God to come and work in our mess but not *that* part of the mess. We want Him to provide us with a new job but not *that* new job. We want Him to restore our marriage but not *that* way. We don't want Him to start working on our selfishness, only on our spouse's selfishness. If we are going to choose to see His glory, that means we are going to choose to follow His way. As Jesus was preparing to perform the most dramatic miracle of His ministry, Martha says, "Wait! Leave the stone. It will smell!" She wants her brother back, but can't Jesus just call on heaven to bring Lazarus out of the tomb minus the burial wrappings and smell? Sure He could, but He doesn't want to address half the mess. He wants to address *all* of it. We think *that* part of our mess is too messy. The smell is just too strong. The situation is too dire. But Jesus reminds Martha and He reminds us that God's glory has never met a mess with an odor that is stronger than the fragrance of heaven. You are not called to stay in your tomb of self-doubt, regret, fear, shame, sorrow, insecurity, or whatever it is you are facing. Jesus removes the stone, steps into the tomb with you, and calls you out of the mess you're in.

Love Is a Sacrifice

One of the major mistakes we make in our understanding of the character of our Father is that we think He doesn't care. It's not that we believe He doesn't care at all, but that the amount of love and care we receive from Him is conditional and not covenantal. We believe that if we run away from God, He won't care enough to pursue us. Even if we've heard a million times that He will leave the ninety-nine to pursue the one, He's God. He has better things to do than chase a screw-up like me. How could God possibly know all of me and still love me? Especially after everything I've done and all the messes I've created. Psalm 33:6 says, "The heavens were made by the word of the LORD, and all the stars, by the breath of his mouth" (CSB). Psalm 139:13 says, "For you created my inmost being; you knit me together in my mother's womb."

By His breath God made the stars in the sky, and He also knit you together in your mother's womb. Have you ever watched someone knit? It's a tedious process! It takes a tremendous amount of care. God spent more time on you than He spent on the stars. He has been caring for you from the start. He cared for you back then, and He cares for you right now. True love isn't measured by what is seen but by what is sacrificed. Love sees all of you—the mess, failures, flaws—and sacrificed the comforts of heaven for the cross of Calvary to bring you home. Jesus didn't say that He would be with you as long as your life is perfectly put together. He said, "I am with you always" (Matthew 28:20).

Maybe you feel a deep longing for a relationship with God. Maybe you've gotten to this point and realized that, somewhere along the way, you miscalculated how much God cares for you and loves you, but now you have a whole new set of questions and problems. How will God react if I try to go back to Him? How do I get home from where I am and have been? Will God even accept me when I show up on His doorstep?

Sons and Daughters, Come on Home

In Luke 15 Jesus teaches through one His most beloved parables, the parable of the prodigal son. We tend to focus on the lost son, but I'm more interested in the father.

Jesus sets the scene by giving us a bit of background knowledge. He says that there was a man who had two sons. The younger son came to the man and asked to receive his inheritance early. The son is basically saying to his father, "Dad, you aren't dying soon enough. I need my share of the inheritance so that I can carry out the plans I have for myself. Unless you plan on dying anytime soon, I'll take my inheritance now. I value it more than I value you." The father gives the son his share of the inheritance, and the son takes his newfound wealth to foreign lands and squanders every cent on foolish living. That brings us to verse 17, where the son begins to recognize the error of his ways: "When he came to his senses, he said, 'How many of my father's hired servants have food to spare, and here I am starving to death! I will set out and go back to my father and say to him: Father, I have sinned against heaven and against you. I am no longer worthy to be called your son; make me like one of your hired servants'" (vv. 17–19).

I think we can relate. The son realizes the mess he's in, and he knows it's a mess that he created. Losing the inheritance was a serious problem. It was an even more serious issue that this young Jewish man lost the inheritance in a foreign land. To live foolishly in Gentile territory brought shame on you, your family, your community, your culture, and your faith. It was an offense that would involve being completely cut off from the community that you once called home. It seemed beyond redemption, but the son wants to go home. He isn't sure what his father will think, but he is pretty certain he will be upset with him, so he prepares a speech. He can't justify what he has done, but he is prepared to take a lesser role in his father's house. He doesn't even care to be called a son. He just wants to be back in his father's home, but look at what happens next.

"He arose and came to his father. But while he was still a long way off, his father saw him and felt compassion, and ran and embraced him and kissed him. And the son said to him, 'Father, I have sinned against heaven and before you. I am no longer worthy to be called your son.' But the father said to his servants, 'Bring quickly the best robe, and put it on him, and put a ring on his hand, and shoes on his feet. And bring the fattened calf and kill it, and let us eat and celebrate'" (vv. 20–23 ESV).

This plays out like a movie in my mind.

After the son comes to his father and asks for the family inheritance, essentially spitting in the face of his father, they gather together at the family table. The father gives the son his share of the inheritance, and he watches his son walk out the door. He tosses and turns all night, weeping for what he has lost—not the money, but his son.

The father has a beautiful home. The best part of the home is the balcony on the roof. It's a spectacular view that sees well over the city gates and out into the wilderness as far as the eye can see. Every morning since his son left, the father has had a routine. He makes a pot of coffee, goes up to the balcony, and prays and thinks about his son. But there is something different about this morning. His heart is particularly heavy and moved by the thought of his son. He gets up a little earlier than usual, before the sun rises. He starts the coffee pot, and once it begins to sputter, he pours himself a cup and makes his way to the balcony. The sun peeks over the mountains in the distance, tears streaming down his face, and he wonders, "Where is he? Is he okay? Is he even alive?" As he looks beyond the city gates, he drops his mug. He sees something unusual.

In the distance he can see a figure making its way toward the city. The father frantically paces the balcony, squinting, trying to make out the identity of the figure. The closer the person gets, he can't make the details of the face out, but he can tell it's a boy. He thinks, "I know that walk. I made that walk. I think that might be him!" As the son comes closer and more into focus, the father can see that it's his hair; he can see that it's him. He's dirty, beat up, and looks broken, but it's him.

As the son approaches the gates, he wonders whether the community will cut him off. He doubts he'll be welcomed home. He's had a long journey, reciting his speech over and over through tears, "Dad, I have sinned against heaven and you. I'm not worthy to be your son. Please take me back. I know don't deserve it. I will be your servant, and I know I don't even deserve that." He looks up through tears as he draws nearer to the city gates, and he sees his father doing something that an older Jewish man is never supposed to do—sprinting toward him. The father runs outside the city gates, and he hugs his son and kisses him. The son starts reciting the speech he practiced, but the father ignores him. He says to his servants, "Get the best robe, a ring for his hand, shoes for his feet, and kill the fattened calf. We're celebrating and throwing the feast of feasts tonight. My son was lost, but now he's found. He is home."

Dr. Ken Bailey points out in his book *The Cross & The Prodigal* that in Jewish culture, men don't run. Why? Because they would have to pull their clothing up to avoid stepping on the end of their garments and tripping. That meant their legs would be exposed, and in their culture that was a shameful thing to do. Why risk bringing shame on yourself? Because, as Dr. Bailey points out, if he didn't, the son would face *keẓaẓah.* Because he had lost the family inheritance in Gentile territory and had the nerve to come back to the community he had left, both the father and the son knew that the community would have performed a ceremony called *keẓaẓah. Keẓaẓah* means "the cutting off," and the ceremony would have consisted of the community breaking a pot at the feet of the son and shouting, "You are now cut off from your people!"[1]

The father ran out to the meet his son because he loved him and felt compassion for him, but also because he wanted to get to his son before the community got to him. Even though the son had made a mess, the father was sure to take on the son's mess as his own. He made sure that the rest of the community knew that his son was welcomed home. The son was right: he was not worthy to be called a son, but he was ready to repent, and the father's compassion and love for his child compelled him to take on the guilt, shame, and sin of his child. The father rejected the idea of his son becoming a servant, and he restored him to sonship.

What is the character of our Father? That while you are still a long way off, He runs to meet you in your mess. You don't need to prepare a speech, and you don't need to worry about taking a lesser role in the eyes of God if you've found yourself wandering. Because of what Jesus did for you on the cross, taking on your guilt, shame, and sin, you are sons and daughters of your Father in heaven. He gave it all to have all of you. He wants to hold you close and call you His. The character of God is that He is rejoicing as you make your way back to Him. He is running out to meet you. God calls Jesus a beloved Son before He does anything to deserve it. He calls you a beloved son or daughter right now.

The Big Reveal

When I was growing up, I remember my mom watching the TV show *Extreme Makeover: Home Edition* every Sunday night. Ty Pennington, his soul patch, and his team, would take underprivileged, tragedy-stricken families, send them off on an incredible vacation, and rebuild their home. When the families returned from vacation, they were treated to an amazing homecoming. They were always driven up to the curb of their new home in a blacked-out suburban or limousine. People who had helped renovate the home, fans of the show, and supporters of the family would line the streets with signs and well-wishes. They anticipated the family's reaction to their new home as much as the family anticipated receiving a new home. The family would get out of the car, but they couldn't see the house yet. A massive bus would block their view.

Ty Pennington would have the family step out of the car, recap their story, and then he, the crowd, and the family would shout, "Bus driver! Move! That! Bus!" The family was always tearful and stunned. And rightfully so—the restoration of these homes was mind-boggling. The big reveal would show the house as it once was and the home that it had become. It didn't seem possible that the renovation was even built on the same foundation, but it was. When they told the bus to move, the emotion that followed wasn't solely based on having an incredible home. It was a representation of what once was and what now is. The last time they had been in their home, it was a place of despair. Now it was a dream come true. What was once an addition to their problems was now a sanctuary of peace. The difference wasn't in the foundation of the home; it was in the work that was put on top of the foundation. Are you ready for the big reveal? Here it is: your mess isn't a sign that you're ruined. When Jesus is your foundation, it's an opportunity for restoration.

Your Mess Matters

In College Station, Texas, it takes a while before the weather cools down in the fall, so when it does, you make the most of your opportunities. My roommate Nate and I lived together from my sophomore year through the time we graduated. The second year we lived together, we ended up renting a house in a residential area about fifteen minutes away from campus. We had to scramble to find a place to live, and this was all we could come up with. It was a perfect, quiet, little one-story place with a small porch on the front. I had no clue what that porch would become. We had church on that porch.

Nate and I developed a routine. Anytime one of us was struggling, we typically sat on the porch for hours on end. We got so familiar with this routine that we would text each other during the day while we were at class, "I need a porch night. You in?"

There was one night when we were both struggling with a multitude of things in our lives. Nate has some significant tragedy in his past, and I had a lot of things I was working through. I was an anxious mess. I was nine hours from family, trying to figure out the whole adulting and manhood thing and trying to grow in my relationship with the Lord and hitting some stumbling blocks. I was also trying to figure out my relationship with my girlfriend at the time (who turned out to be my wife), which was harder than trying to figure out my relationship with God. Some nights the stress and anxiety were overwhelming, and on this particular night, we were both opening up about everything. We choked back tears all night.

After we hadn't said much in a while, I remember checking the time on my phone and saying, "Well, I have class in five hours, so I guess I should try to get a few hours of sleep."

"I'm probably not going to class," Nate responded. He smiled and motioned that he was about to head inside. "One day I think God will help us understand how this all makes sense, Luke."

I nodded in agreement and put a finger to my lips to remind him to stay quiet. In the top corner of the porch, where the porch and the house met, there was a family of swallows that had made their nest, and they would sleep right above us. I looked up there to make sure we hadn't woke them, but they were still sound asleep. I believe God put that family of swallows there to remind us of what Jesus said in Matthew 6, "Therefore I tell you, do not worry about your life, what you will eat or drink; or about your body, what you will wear. Is not life more than food, and the body more than clothes? Look at the birds of the air; they do not sow or reap or store away in barns, and yet your heavenly Father feeds them. Are you not much more valuable than they?" (vv. 25–26).

"I think it will all make sense one day too, Nate," I responded. We started shuffling into the house and were about to go our separate ways when I said, "Who knows? Maybe I'll write a book about it someday."

Too often we look at the messes in our lives as an impossible gap to traverse, but the bridge between where you are right now and where you know you need to be is the cross of Jesus Christ, and it has been paved by His blood. The gospel itself is messy. It's a story marked by dirt from the beginning, the blood of an innocent man, and the tears of a loving Father. It's a story marked by suffering, forgiveness, brokenness, and redemption. Your story starts and ends with a mess, with Jesus pouring Himself out for you on a rugged cross. This poem beautifully illustrates this idea:

> For you He walked along the path of woe,
> He was sharply struck with His head bent low.
> He knew the deepest sorrow, pain, and grief,
> He knew long endurance with no relief,
> He took all the bitter from death's deep cup,
> He kept no blood drops but gave them all up.
> Yes, for you, and for me, He won the fight
> To take us to glory and realms of light.[2]
>
> L. S. P.

God knows your deepest pains and most abominable messes. Jesus put it succinctly: "It is not those who are healthy who need a doctor, but those who are sick" (Luke 5:31 CSB). In other words, He didn't come to avoid your mess. He came to step into it. The messes in your life aren't a sore subject for Him. There is no point in hiding something from someone who knows where it's hidden. He isn't calling you to dress anything up or to bury it; He is restoring it and calling it to rise. He isn't the Great Mortician; He's the Great Physician.

My prayer is that you won't settle for the comfort of knowing that God knows about your deep pains and abominable messes but that you would walk in the uncomfortable calling of allowing God to use them. Pain may be pointless, and messes may be meaningless, but not if we ask God to reveal their purpose and meaning to us. He can and will use them for your good and His glory. Heaven shouted down for the angel to move the stone in front of Jesus's tomb, and God revealed restoration in the form of resurrection.

Augustine is often credited as saying, "There is no saint without a past, no sinner without a future."[3] We all have a story, and all stories feature highs and lows. We each have messes in our past, present, and future. Your life is an ongoing story, and in all the messes you have encountered or will encounter in the future, God promises to meet you in every single one.

When I was in the middle of my health crisis, I felt like I was alone, but I wasn't alone. I only felt that way because I didn't like what God was doing in it. As I was in the middle of that mess, I felt like God had left me in the valley, but really He was dragging me out of a few valleys you may be familiar with—the valleys of self-reliance, pride, and anger, to name a few. He used my illness to instill an incontrovertible truth within me: that God was for me, even if that meant my feeling like He was against me. It was in that mess, not before or after, but *in* that mess, that God taught me to trust Him. Because God loves me, He was committed to making me into who He had called me to be, even if that upset me at times. I tried to run away, but He kept pursuing.

Everything I am and everything I'm becoming can be traced back to that mess. If life happens in acts, that is where a new act began. Rather than pretending to be someone I wish I were, I was able to begin to move toward who God was preparing me to be. It was a mess, but God has worked a miracle, and He can do the same with you. I'm by no means a finished product—I need His grace every moment of every day—but I know that Jesus is faithful to sustain me in every mess.

When messes inevitably come up in your life, you don't have to avoid them. Leap boldly and confidently into the heart of the mess, with unwavering trust in Jesus, who will meet you in it and walk with you through it. As intimidating and devastating as the messiness of life can be, it is nothing compared with the confidence and security you can feel in knowing that your mess matters to God, and nothing can stand against the wonders of His power and grace.

There is water to walk on, crosses to carry, and eternity to press into. We have our fair share of messes and miracles. Above all, though, we have Jesus Christ, and with Him and through Him, all things are possible. My prayer is that you would know in your deepest being that you aren't made of the mess; you're made in the mess. And it matters more than you can imagine.

Notes

Chapter 1: Made in the Mess

1. Rebecca Beatrice Brooks, "The British Army in The Revolutionary War," November 27, 2017, https://historyofmassachusetts.org/british-army-revolutionary-war/.
2. Eric Trickey, "The Prussian Nobleman Who Helped Save the American Revolution," *When American troops faltered, Baron von Stueben helped whip them into shape*, April 26, 2017, https://www.smithsonianmag.com/history/baron-von-steuben-180963048/.
3. "General von Steuben," Last updated February 3, 2016, https://www.nps.gov/vafo/learn/historyculture/vonsteuben.htm (February 27, 2019).
4. "General von Steuben," Last updated February 3, 2016. https://www.nps.gov/vafo/learn/historyculture/vonsteuben.htm (February 27, 2019).
5. Eric Trickey, "The Prussian Nobleman Who Helped Save the American Revolution," *When American troops faltered, Baron von Stueben*

helped whip them into shape, April 26, 2017, https://www.smithsonianmag.com/history/baron-von-steuben-180963048/.

6. J. K. Rowling, *Harry Potter and the Chamber of Secrets* (London: Bloomsbury, 1998), 333.
7. "A Quote by Søren Kierkegaard," *Forbes*, https://www.forbes.com/quotes/8761/.

Chapter 2: The Soil You Despise

1. Carl Rosen, Department of Soil, Water, and Climate, last updated September 16, 2015, https://www.swac.umn.edu/directory/faculty/carl-rosen.
2. Carl J. Rosen and Peter M. Bierman, "Nutrient Management for Fruit and Vegetable Crop Production: Using Manure and Compost as Nutrient Sources for Vegetable Crops," 2005, retrieved from the University of Minnesota Digital Conservancy, http://hdl.handle.net/11299/200639.
3. Martha Stewart Living, "Rose Growing Guide," 2005, https://www.marthastewart.com/268915/rose-growing-guide.
4. L. B. Cowman, *Streams in the Desert* (Grand Rapids: Zondervan, 1997), 279.

Chapter 4: The Gift of Pain and How to Press through It

1. Justin Heckert, "The Hazards of Growing Up Painlessly," *New York Times*, November 15, 2012, https://www.nytimes.com/2012/11/18/magazine/ashlyn-blocker-feels-no-pain.html.
2. Justin Heckert, "The Hazards of Growing Up Painlessly," *New York Times*, November 15, 2012, https://www.nytimes.com/2012/11/18/magazine/ashlyn-blocker-feels-no-pain.html.
3. L. B. Cowman, *Streams in the Desert*, September 19, updated edition (Grand Rapids: Zondervan, 1997), 357.
4. Charles H. Spurgeon, *The Devotional Classics of C. H. Spurgeon*, Volume 1 of the Twelve Volume Set (Lafayette, IN: Sovereign Grace Publishers, 1990), 303.

5. A quote by Ian Bottomley, "Forging a Katana (Japanese Samurai Sword)," YouTube, November 27, 2012, https://www.youtube.com/watch?v=VE_4zHNcieM.
6. Cathy Chester, "A Path To Healing: The Wound Is the Place Where the Light Enters You," last updated December 6, 2017, *Huffington Post*, https://www.huffingtonpost.com/cathy-chester/a-path-to-healing-the-wou_b_7916968.html.

Chapter 5: You Can't Win the War on Your Own

1. Oswald Chambers, *My Utmost for His Highest*, "The Relinquished Life," March 8, https://utmost.org/classic/the-relinquished-life-classic/.

Chapter 6: Hanging on by a Thread

1. "Quotes," IMDb, https://www.imdb.com/title/tt0167261/characters/nm0000704.

Chapter 7: The King of Thieves

1. Everette A. James et. al., "Brain Institute," *Using Lots of Social Media Sites Raises Depression Risk*, Brain Institute, University of Pittsburgh, http://www.braininstitute.pitt.edu/using-lots-social-media-sites-raises-depression-risk.
2. Elizabeth Hoge, David Bickham, and Joanne Cantor, "Digital Media, Anxiety, and Depression in Children," *Pediatrics*, November 01, 2017, http://pediatrics.aappublications.org/content/140/Supplement_2/S76?utm_source=TrendMD&utm_medium=TrendMD&utm_campaign=Pediatrics_TrendMD_0.
3. David Sanderson, "Why Do Horses Wear Blinders?" Dallas Equestrian Center, June 25, 2014, http://www.dallasequestriancenter.com/why-do-horses-wear-blinders/).
4. Dhwty, "Raphael: A Renaissance Artist More Versatile than Michelangelo and More Prolific than Leonardo?" *Ancient*

Origins, April 29, 2017, https://www.ancient-origins.net/history-famous-people/raphael-renaissance-artist-more-versatile-michelangelo-and-more-prolific-021365.

5. Allyssia Alleyne, "Painting Bought for $25 Could Be $26m Raphael," *CNN*, November 11, 2016, https://www.cnn.com/style/article/painting-bought-for-25-dollars-could-be-an-original-raphael/index.html.
6. Curtis E. Doris and Curtis C. Bryan, *Inspirational Thoughts to Warm the Soul: Quotations, Stories, and More* (Bloomington, IN: iUniverse, 2011), 189.
7. Spurgeon, Charles Haddon, "The Evils of the Present Time, and Our Object, Necessities, and Encouragements" *The Treasury of David*, https://archive.spurgeon.org/misc/aarm10.php.

Chapter 8: Burn through the Night

1. Elie Wiesel, *"Create Change,"* Elie Wiesel Foundation, http://eliewieselfoundation.org/news/visit-to-buchenwald/.
2. "Apathy," Oxford Dictionaries, https://en.oxforddictionaries.com/definition/apathy.

Chapter 9: From Mess to Masterpiece

1. "Michelangelo's David: Admire World's Greatest Sculpture at Accademia Gallery," Guide to Accademia Gallery, http://www.accademia.org/explore-museum/artworks/michelangelos-david/.
2. "Altered Images," Smithsonian, https://www.smithsonianmag.com/photocontest/detail/altered-images/there-is-strong-shadow-where-there-is-much-light-johann-wolfgang-von-goethe/.
3. "Quotes," IMDb, https://www.imdb.com/title/tt1345836/quotes/?tab=qt&ref_=tt_trv_qu.

Chapter 10: The Art of Remembering

1. Brian Dunbar, "July 20, 1969: One Giant Leap for Mankind," NASA, last updated January 31, 2019, https://www.nasa.gov/mission_pages/apollo/apollo11.html.
2. Dave Mosher, "The American Flags on the Moon Are Disintegrating," *Business Insider*, April 9, 2017, https://www.businessinsider.com/american-flags-moon-color-bleached-white-2017-4.

Chapter 11: By the Blood

1. Oswald Chambers, *My Utmost for His Highest*, "His Agony and Our Access," April 5, https://utmost.org/his-agony-and-our-access/.

Chapter 12: Bring the Broken Home

1. Kenneth E. Bailey, *The Cross & the Prodigal: Luke 15 through the Eyes of Middle Eastern Peasants* (Downers Grove, IL: InterVarsity Press, 2005), 52–53.
2. L. B. Cowman and James Reimann, *Streams in the Desert: 366 Daily Devotional Readings.* (Grand Rapids: Zondervan, 2013), 378.
3. Bobby Schuller, *You Are Beloved: Living in the Freedom of God's Grace, Mercy, and Love* (Nashville: Thomas Nelson, 2018), 8.